KB174644

Fundamental Reading

Michael A. Putlack
Stephen Poirier
Tony Covello

PLUS 3

DARAKWON

Fundamental Reading PLUS 3

Publisher Chung Kyudo
Authors Michael A. Putlack, Stephen Poirier, Tony Covello
Editors Jeong Yeonsoon, Kim Minju, Kim Namyeon
Designers Park Narae, Elim

First published in January 2020
By Darakwon, Inc.
Darakwon Bldg., 211, Munbal-ro, Paju-si, Gyeonggi-do 10881
Republic of Korea
Tel: 82-2-736-2031 (Ext. 250)
Fax: 82-2-732-2037

ISBN 978-89-277-0861-2 54740
978-89-277-0856-8 54740 (set)

www.darakwon.co.kr

Photo Credits
Music4mix (p. 11), Photo Oz (p. 12), Blulz60 (p. 13), Renata Sedmakova (p. 16),
serato (p. 19), VDB Photos (p. 33) / www.shutterstock.com
Web Gallery of Art (p. 18), File:Wga 12c illuminated manuscripts Mary
Magdalen announcing the resurrection.jpg / https://commons.wikimedia.org/
wiki/

Components Main Book / Workbook
10 9 8 7 6 5 4   23 24 25 26 27

Fundamental Reading

PLUS **3**

DARAKWON

How to Use This Book

This book has 8 chapters that cover different academic subjects. Each chapter is composed of 2 units based on interesting topics related to the subject.

Student Book

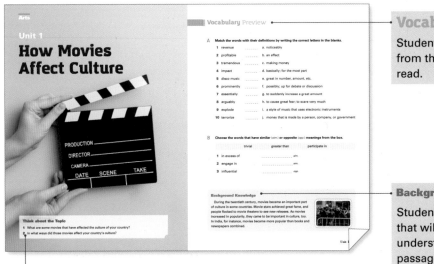

Think about the Topic
Two warm-up questions are provided to motivate students to think about the topic before continuing with the unit.

Vocabulary Preview
Students can learn the key words from the passage and get ready to read.

Background Knowledge
Students can read brief information that will help them predict and understand the main reading passage.

QR code for listening to the passage

Main Reading Passage
The passages discuss topics that have been carefully chosen to provide academic knowledge as well as to interest students. Each passage is between 320–350 words long.

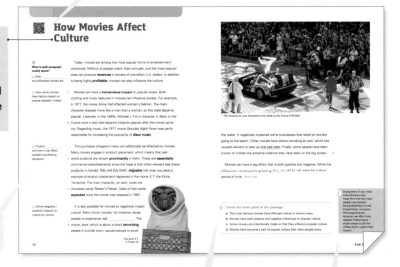

Finding the topic of each paragraph

Finding the main topic or main idea of the passage

Additional information and further learning about the topic

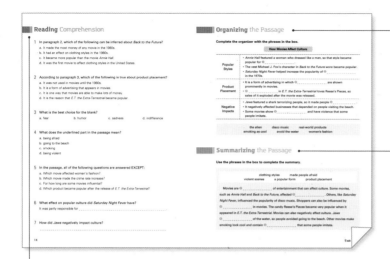

Reading Comprehension

5 multiple-choice questions and 2 short-answer questions are given to help students master various types of questions.

Organizing the Passage

By completing a graphic organizer or a Fill in a Table question, students can review and recognize important ideas and information presented in the passage.

Summarizing the Passage

By completing a regular summary or a Prose Summary question, students can review the main points of the passage once again.

TOEFL Practice Test

At the end of the book, there is a supplementary TOEFL Practice Test section containing four passages. Each passage has six questions similar to ones that frequently appear on real TOEFL tests.

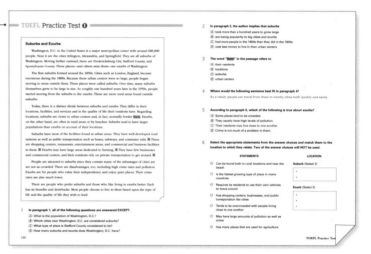

Workbook

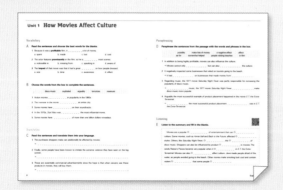

The first part contains 4 types of exercises, which provide students with a deeper understanding of the passage as well as enhanced vocabulary and language skills.

The second part presents a writing topic related to the reading passage. Students can develop their thoughts on the topic, conduct further research on their own, and learn to write a short paragraph.

Table of Contents

Chapter 1
Arts

The arts refer to the study of creative disciplines such as art, music, theater, drama, and film. Artists engage in the formation of physical representations of their creative minds. Thus they may make paintings, drawings, songs, plays, movies, TV programs, and other similar types of creative pieces.

Unit 1
How Movies Affect Culture

Think about the Topic

1 What are some movies that have affected the culture of your country?

2 In what ways did those movies affect your country's culture?

Vocabulary Preview

A   **Match the words with their definitions by writing the correct letters in the blanks.**

1 revenue	_____	a. noticeably
2 profitable	_____	b. an effect
3 tremendous	_____	c. making money
4 impact	_____	d. basically; for the most part
5 disco music	_____	e. great in number, amount, etc.
6 prominently	_____	f. possibly; up for debate or discussion
7 essentially	_____	g. to suddenly increase a great amount
8 arguably	_____	h. to cause great fear; to scare very much
9 explode	_____	i. a style of music that uses electronic instruments
10 terrorize	_____	j. money that is made by a person, company, or government

B   **Choose the words that have similar (*sim.*) or opposite (*opp.*) meanings from the box.**

trivial	greater than	participate in

1 in excess of   _____ *sim.*

2 engage in   _____ *sim.*

3 influential   _____ *opp.*

Background Knowledge

During the twentieth century, movies became an important part of culture in some countries. Movie stars achieved great fame, and people flocked to movie theaters to see new releases. As movies increased in popularity, they came to be important in culture, too. In India, for instance, movies became more popular than books and newspapers combined.

How Movies Affect Culture

Q

What is each paragraph mainly about?

P1 How _____ and influential movies are

P2 How some movies have had an impact on popular (people / styles)

P3 Product _____ and how it can affect people's purchasing decisions

P4 Some (negative / positive) impacts on culture by movies

Today, movies are among the most popular forms of entertainment worldwide. Millions of people watch them annually, and the most popular ones can produce **revenues** in excess of one billion U.S. dollars. In addition to being highly **profitable**, movies can also influence the culture.

5   Movies can have a **tremendous impact** on popular styles. Both clothing and music featured in movies can influence society. For example, in 1977, the movie *Annie Hall* affected women's fashion. The main character dressed more like a man than a woman, so this style became popular. Likewise, in the 1980s, Michael J. Fox's character in *Back to the* 10 *Future* wore a vest that became instantly popular after the movie came out. Regarding music, the 1977 movie *Saturday Night Fever* was partly responsible for increasing the popularity of **disco music**.

  The purchases shoppers make can additionally be affected by movies. Many movies engage in product placement, which means that real- 15 world products are shown **prominently** in them. These are **essentially** commercial advertisements since the hope is that when viewers see these products in movies, they will buy them. **Arguably** the most successful example of product placement happened in the movie *E.T. the Extra- Terrestrial*. The main character, an alien, loves the 20 chocolate candy Reese's Pieces. Sales of that candy **exploded** once the movie was released in 1982.

  It is also possible for movies to negatively impact culture. Many horror movies, for instance, cause people to experience real _____. The 25 movie *Jaws*, which is about a shark **terrorizing** people in a small town, caused people to avoid

▶ The alien E.T.
© Photo Oz

▲ The famous car and characters from *Back to the Future* © Blulz60

the water. It negatively impacted some businesses that relied on tourists going to the beach. Other movies have shown smoking as cool, which has caused viewers to take up <u>that bad habit</u>. Finally, some people have been known to imitate the extreme violence they have seen on the big screen. ₃₀

Movies can have a big effect that is both positive and negative. While the effects are not always long lasting, they can still be influential for a short period of time. Words 338

During times of war, many movie directors have made films that help make people more patriotic. During World War II in the United States, numerous films supporting the American war effort were released. These helped inspire people to join the military and to support their country.

 Check the main point of the passage.

a. The most famous movies have affected culture in various ways.

b. Movies have both positive and negative influences on popular culture.

c. Some movies are intentionally made so that they influence popular culture.

d. Movies have become a part of popular culture that many people enjoy.

Reading Comprehension

1 In paragraph 2, which of the following can be inferred about *Back to the Future*?

   a. It made the most money of any movie in the 1980s.

   b. It had an effect on clothing styles in the 1980s.

   c. It became more popular than the movie *Annie Hall*.

   d. It was the first movie to affect clothing styles in the United States.

2 According to paragraph 3, which of the following is true about product placement?

   a. It was not used in movies until the 1980s.

   b. It is a form of advertising that appears in movies.

   c. It is one way that movies are able to make lots of money.

   d. It is the reason that *E.T. the Extra-Terrestrial* became popular.

3 What is the best choice for the blank?

   a. fear   b. humor   c. sadness   d. indifference

4 What does the underlined part in the passage mean?

   a. being afraid

   b. going to the beach

   c. smoking

   d. being violent

5 In the passage, all of the following questions are answered EXCEPT:

   a. Which movie affected women's fashion?

   b. Which movie made the crime rate increase?

   c. For how long are some movies influential?

   d. Which product became popular after the release of *E.T. the Extra-Terrestrial*?

6 What effect on popular culture did *Saturday Night Fever* have?

   It was partly responsible for _____ .

7 How did *Jaws* negatively impact culture?

   _____

Organizing the Passage

Complete the organizer with the phrases in the box.

	How Movies Affect Culture
Popular Styles	• *Annie Hall* featured a woman who dressed like a man, so that style became popular for ❶_____. • The vest Michael J. Fox's character in *Back to the Future* wore became popular. • *Saturday Night Fever* helped increase the popularity of ❷_____ in the 1970s.
Product Placement	• It is a form of advertising in which ❸_____ are shown prominently in movies. • ❹_____ in *E.T. the Extra-Terrestrial* loves Reese's Pieces, so sales of it exploded after the movie was released.
Negative Impacts	• *Jaws* featured a shark terrorizing people, so it made people ❺_____. • It negatively affected businesses that depended on people visiting the beach. • Some movies show ❻_____ and have violence that some people imitate.

the alien	disco music	real-world products
smoking as cool	avoid the water	women's fashion

Summarizing the Passage

Use the phrases in the box to complete the summary.

clothing styles		made people afraid
violent scenes	a popular form	product placement

Movies are ❶_____ of entertainment that can affect culture. Some movies, such as *Annie Hall* and *Back to the Future*, affected ❷_____. Others, like *Saturday Night Fever*, influenced the popularity of disco music. Shoppers can also be influenced by ❸_____ in movies. The candy Reese's Pieces became very popular when it appeared in *E.T. the Extra-Terrestrial*. Movies can also negatively affect culture. *Jaws* ❹_____ of the water, so people avoided going to the beach. Other movies make smoking look cool and contain ❺_____ that some people imitate.

Unit 2
Painting Techniques of the Renaissance

Think about the Topic

1 What was the Renaissance?

2 What are some painting techniques that artists use on their works?

Vocabulary Preview

A **Match the words with their definitions by writing the correct letters in the blanks.**

1 rebirth _____ a. exactness

2 reintroduce _____ b. greatly; very much

3 dramatically _____ c. shade; darkness

4 spiritual _____ d. to show; to portray

5 fresco _____ e. the topic of a work of art

6 subject matter _____ f. the act of being born again

7 depict _____ g. to start using something again

8 shadow _____ h. relating to the soul or something religious

9 precision _____ i. a type of art in which the artist paints on wet plaster

10 scale _____ j. a ratio between the size of something real and the size of
something showing it

B **Choose the words that have similar** (*sim.*) **or opposite** (*opp.*) **meanings from the box.**

abstract	method	copy

1 realistic _____ *opp.*

2 imitate _____ *sim.*

3 technique _____ *sim.*

Background Knowledge

During the Middle Ages, most knowledge from ancient Greece
and Rome was lost in the West. However, it was preserved in
the East by the Byzantine Empire. In the 1300s and 1400s, many
Byzantine scholars fled the empire because the Ottoman Turks were
attacking the empire. They went to Italy and took their knowledge
with them. This helped begin the Renaissance in the West.

Painting Techniques of the Renaissance

Q

What is each paragraph mainly about?

P1 When the Renaissance lasted and (how / what) happened during it

P2 The characteristics of art in the _____

P3 How artists used _____ from ancient Greece and Rome during the Renaissance

P4 Some art _____ used during the Renaissance

The Renaissance was a period of time in Europe which lasted from approximately 1400 to 1600. It began in Italy and then spread to other parts of Europe. During it, there was a **rebirth** of learning in numerous fields. Among them were the sciences, engineering, and the arts. Because of the
5 knowledge that was **reintroduced**, the way many artists painted changed **dramatically**.

The Middle Ages was the period that came before the Renaissance. It was a **spiritual** age, so most of the art was religious in nature. Murals
10 and **frescoes** of scenes from the Bible decorated church walls. Stained-glass windows in churches and cathedrals were also common sights. Many artists spent time drawing pictures in books, too. Most of the artwork done in the Middle Ages was
15 flat and two dimensional. It had no depth, and the images, especially the people in it, were not always realistic.

▲ A painting from the Middle Ages

This changed when the Renaissance began. One feature of that period was that people began to relearn knowledge from ancient Greece and Rome that had been lost over time. Artists began to imitate the styles used
20 centuries ago. One change concerned **subject matter**. The Renaissance was an age of humanism, so artwork did not always focus on religious themes. Instead, regular people or characters from mythology were **depicted**. The images of them looked very realistic as well.

In addition, the techniques artists used changed. For example, artists
25 used a painting method called perspective to give their works a three-dimensional appearance. They emphasized the uses of **shadows** and

▲ *The School of Athens* by Raphael

light to bring life to their paintings. They also began utilizing mathematical **precision** in their works. In the Middle Ages, people in paintings could often appear to be much larger than they were in reality. Renaissance painters made sure that what they painted was drawn to **scale**. This made *30* their works look more realistic.

Among the greatest artists of the Renaissance were Michelangelo, Leonardo da Vinci, Raphael, and Botticelli. Their work owes a great deal to the knowledge that came from ancient Rome and Greece. Words 339

📑 (Where / Who) some famous Renaissance artists were

ⓘ A fresco is a type of mural, a wall painting. To make a fresco, an artist places wet plaster onto a wall or ceiling. Then, before the plaster dries, the artist paints on it. To enlarge the fresco, the artist adds additional bits of plaster and paints on them.

 Check what the passage is mainly about.

a. The rebirth of learning that happened during the Renaissance

b. The best artists of the Renaissance and their painting techniques

c. The Renaissance and the reasons that it started in Italy in the 1400s

d. Various painting methods artists learned to use during the Renaissance

Unit 2   19

Reading Comprehension

1 In paragraph 1, which of the following is NOT mentioned about the Renaissance?

   a. The period of time when it lasted

   b. The reason there was a rebirth of knowledge

   c. The fields where there was a rebirth in learning

   d. The place where it began and where it spread to

2 The word scenes in the passage is closest in meaning to

   a. characters   b. locations   c. things   d. events

3 Which of the following is true about art in the Middle Ages?

   a. It focused on both nature and humans.

   b. It was influenced by ancient Greece and Rome.

   c. The images created during it were vivid and realistic.

   d. It was often seen on the walls or windows of churches and cathedrals.

4 The word they in the passage refers to

   a. the uses of shadows and light

   b. their works

   c. the Middle Ages

   d. people in paintings

5 According to paragraph 4, which of the following is true about perspective?

   a. It was first used by artists during the Middle Ages.

   b. It lets artists make their works more three dimensional.

   c. It requires artists to use mathematical precision.

   d. It involves the usage of both shadows and light in painting.

6 What did artwork during the Renaissance focus on?

It often depicted _____ .

7 Who were some of the greatest artists of the Renaissance?

_____

Organizing the Passage

Select the appropriate statements from the answer choices and match them to the period to which they relate. Two of the answer choices will NOT be used.

Middle Ages	Renaissance
•	•
•	•
	•

1 Had artists that used perspective, shadows and light, and mathematical precision

2 Focused on humanist topics and had regular people and mythological characters depicted

3 Was a spiritual age in which most art featured religious topics

4 Was the longest-lasting age in the past two thousand years

5 Brought about a rebirth in learning from ancient Greece and Rome

6 Started in Italy and then only affected that area for around two hundred years

7 Had artists who created flat and two-dimensional art

Summarizing the Passage

Use the phrases in the box to complete the summary.

look three dimensional   mathematical precision
ancient Greece and Rome   period of relearning   religious art

The Renaissance was a ❶_____ that lasted from around 1400 to 1600. The Middle Ages happened before the Renaissance. It was a spiritual age, and artists mostly created ❷_____ that was flat and two dimensional. The Renaissance used knowledge relearned from ❸_____. It was an age of humanism, so regular people and characters from mythology were depicted. Artists used different techniques, too. Perspective made their works ❹_____. They also used shadows and light as well as ❺_____.

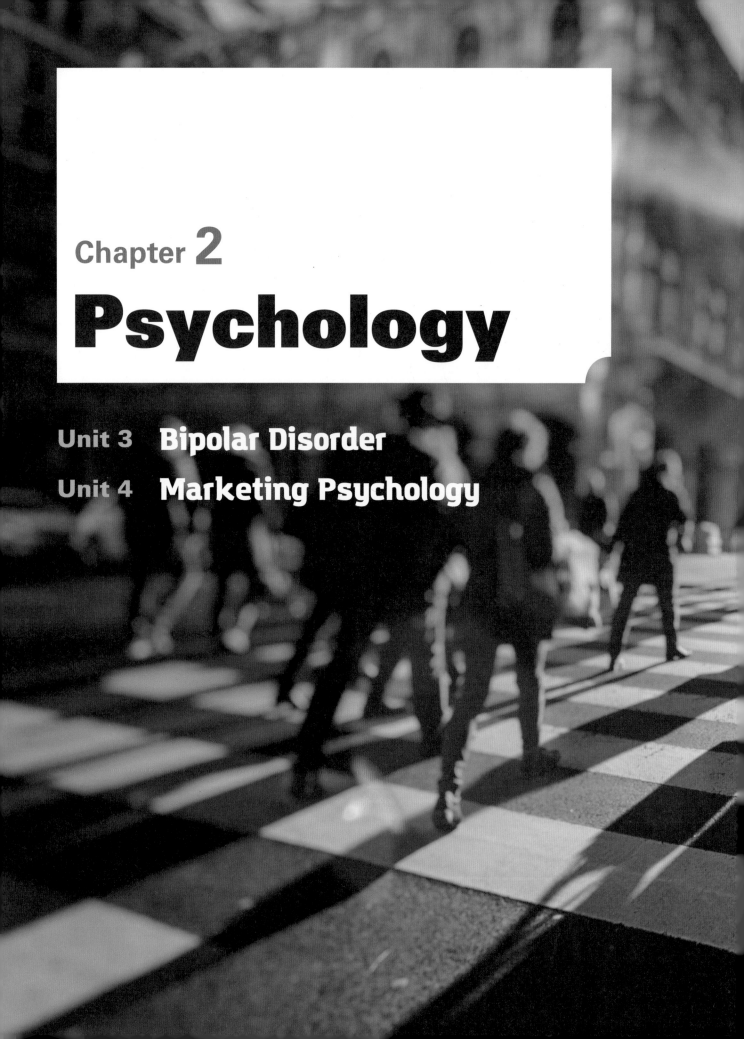

Chapter 2
Psychology

Psychology refers to the study of the mind and behavior. Psychologists try to understand how people think, act, and feel and understand why they act in certain ways. Some psychologists assist people in dealing with various mental problems they have. These include issues such as depression, suicidal feelings, and more severe mental problems.

Unit 3

Bipolar Disorder

Think about the Topic

1 What are some psychological problems people have?

2 How can psychological problems be treated?

Vocabulary Preview

A **Match the words with their definitions by writing the correct letters in the blanks.**

1 psychiatrist _____   a. the act of killing oneself

2 mood swing _____   b. to make constant or steady

3 suicide _____   c. to focus on or think about very much

4 concentrate _____   d. to do something as a final solution

5 imbalance _____   e. a doctor who treats people with mental problems

6 cure (*n.*) _____   f. to officially say what medicine or treatment a patient needs

7 resort to _____   g. the state of something not being in the right proportions

8 prescribe _____   h. a method of healing or returning a person to health

9 stabilize _____   i. a sudden development or discovery of great importance

10 breakthrough _____   j. the change of a person's feelings from happiness to sadness

B **Choose the words that have similar (*sim.*) or opposite (*opp.*) meanings from the box.**

illness	upset	undergo

1 experience   _____ *sim.*

2 disorder   _____ *sim.*

3 stabilize   _____ *opp.*

Background Knowledge

There are many mental disorders people may have. Among them are depression, anxiety, eating disorders, and addictive behaviors. Large numbers of people do not recognize the symptoms of certain disorders, so they never seek treatment. However, a lot of mental disorders can be overcome through a combination of medicine and behavioral changes.

Bipolar Disorder

Q

What is each paragraph mainly about?

P1 How bipolar disorder (cures / affects) people

P2 _____ symptoms of bipolar disorder

P3 Possible (causes / effects) of bipolar disorder

P4 Common ways to _____ bipolar disorder

Psychiatrists have identified a large number of mental problems people suffer from. Bipolar disorder is one such condition that affects many people. In the United States alone, it is estimated that roughly six million people suffer from it each year. Individuals with bipolar disorder experience **mood**

5 **swings** that make them feel anywhere from being very happy to being very sad. If untreated, the condition can cause problems for people at their jobs and in their relationships. In some cases, it can even lead to **suicide**.

Some of the most common symptoms of it are thinking and talking quickly, changing one's mind almost instantly, and an inability to

10 **concentrate**. People with bipolar disorder also frequently have trouble sleeping, become angry easily, and make poor decisions. A person may have all, some, or just a couple of these symptoms. Because the symptoms are common ones many healthy people have, there are some individuals who go untreated for years.

15 The cause of bipolar disorder has not yet been determined. There are some who believe it is caused by an **imbalance** in the brain's *hormone levels. Others claim that stress and a person's lifestyle can cause it. In most people, it appears in their late teens or early twenties. There is no known **cure**, but it can be controlled.

20 The most common treatments are lifestyle changes and medication. Doctors encourage patients to decrease the amount of stress in their lives. They are also recommended to plan activities they enjoy to get a sense of fulfillment. Getting more exercise and sleeping enough can _____ the

25 symptoms of bipolar disorder, too. So can a healthy diet.

Nevertheless, a large number of people must **resort to** taking medication. Lithium is often **prescribed**. It can **stabilize** people's mood swings yet cannot eliminate them. However, many sufferers believe the medicine has made them better, so they stop taking it after a while. Their symptoms then ³⁰ quickly reappear.

Until a **breakthrough** is made, millions of people will suffer from this issue every year. Their only hope until that occurs is to live healthy lives and to take medication with regularity. Words 350

*hormone: a compound created in the body that may affect the function of a certain organ or bodily tissue

P5 How _____ can help people with bipolar disorder

i Lithium is able to reduce the occurrence and severity of problems for people with bipolar disorder. People taking it are less likely to kill themselves. They are also less likely to suffer from depression.

 Check what the passage is mainly about.

a. The most serious mental disorders and their cures

b. Some new theories on the treatment of bipolar disorder

c. The reasons that most people with bipolar disorder have it

d. The symptoms of bipolar disorder and how it can be treated

---

Reading Comprehension

1 In paragraph 1, which of the following is mentioned about bipolar disorder?

    a. What emotions people with it may experience

    b. How many people with it commit suicide

    c. What psychiatrists can do for people who have it

    d. How common it is compared to other mental disorders

2 According to paragraph 2, which of the following is NOT true about the symptoms of bipolar disorder?

    a. It can cause people to have anger issues.

    b. Some people with it may change their minds quickly.

    c. Some people may feel like eating more than normal.

    d. It may cause people to be unable to sleep well.

3 In paragraph 3, which of the following can be inferred about bipolar disorder?

    a. It might be caused by some people's own actions.

    b. People who are in their thirties never suffer from it.

    c. Doctors believe they will never cure it in the future.

    d. It is more affected by the brain's hormone levels than by stress.

4 What is the best choice for the blank?

    a. delete   b. reduce   c. do nothing to   d. worsen

5 Why does the author mention Lithium?

    a. To claim it has cured people with bipolar disorder

    b. To name a medicine used to treat bipolar disorder

    c. To argue that it can worsen the symptoms of bipolar disorder

    d. To point out that few people like taking it for bipolar disorder

6 How many people suffer from bipolar disorder in the United States?

    It is estimated that _____.

7 What are the two most common treatments for bipolar disorders?

    _____

Organizing the Passage

Complete the organizer with the phrases in the box.

Bipolar Disorder	
Symptoms	• People may experience ❶_____. • Sufferers think and talk quickly, change their minds instantly, and cannot concentrate. • They may have trouble sleeping, become angry easily, and ❷_____.
Causes	• Some believe an imbalance in the brain's ❸_____ causes it. • Others think stress and ❹_____ can cause it.
Treatments	• Patients are encouraged to decrease ❺_____, to exercise, and to sleep enough. • Some resort to taking medication ❻_____.

mood swings	such as lithium	make poor decisions
hormone levels	their stress levels	a person's lifestyle

Summarizing the Passage

Use the phrases in the box to complete the summary.

	job and relationship	stop taking it
change their lifestyles	sleep enough	think and talk

There are many mental problems people suffer from, and bipolar disorder is one of them. It can cause mood swings in people and cause ❶_____ problems, too. Some of its symptoms are to make people ❷_____ quickly and to change their minds instantly. Its causes could be a hormone imbalance or lifestyle issues. To treat it, people are encouraged to ❸_____ and to take medication. People should reduce their stress, exercise, and ❹_____. Lithium can help, but people's symptoms reappear if they ❺_____.

Unit 4

Marketing Psychology

Vocabulary Preview

A **Match the words with their definitions by writing the correct letters in the blanks.**

1 market (v.) _____   a. a purpose

2 sophisticated _____   b. an advantage

3 edge _____   c. rashly; without thinking

4 impulsively _____   d. complex or advanced

5 cash register _____   e. to go to or gather in large numbers

6 intention _____   f. a plan designed to gain an advantage

7 bandwagon _____   g. the exchange of something between people

8 reciprocity _____   h. a cause or movement that attracts many people

9 ploy _____   i. to promote a good or service to make people buy it

10 flock _____   j. a machine that records individual sales and is used for storing money

B **Choose the words that have similar** (sim.) **or opposite** (opp.) **meanings from the box.**

feature	vendor	commercial

1 advertisement _____ sim.

2 consumer _____ opp.

3 aspect _____ sim.

Background Knowledge

People and businesses have been marketing their goods and services for centuries. Many times, they simply use signs showing what is for sale. In more recent times, it has become possible to advertise on television, radio, and the Internet as well as in print publications. Some people and businesses are starting to use psychology to learn how to market their goods and services better.

Marketing Psychology

Q

What is each paragraph mainly about?

P1 What marketing is and how some _____ use it

P2 How businesses market to people who act _____

P3 (Where / What) the bandwagon effect is

P4 How (reciprocity / tipping) is used in marketing

Once a business has a good or service to sell, it is necessary to **market** it. Marketing refers to the art of convincing consumers to purchase a good or service. Many businesses use simple advertisements that describe whatever they are selling. Yet nowadays, some are resorting to more

5 **sophisticated** methods by using marketing psychology. A key aspect of it is to try to understand the consumer. By using marketing psychology, businesses hope to get an **edge** over their competition.

One important fact that psychologists know is that consumers tend to act **impulsively**. Many people make purchases without thinking. For

10 instance, supermarkets almost always place shelves of items for sale near the **cash registers**. People waiting in line may notice these items and, on impulse, add them to their shopping carts. They had no **intention** of buying them when they entered the store. But they still acquire them.

People also desire what others have. This is the **bandwagon**

15 effect. In advertising, businesses often use colorful images. The ads show happy, smiling people using their products. The message being sent is that if these people are happy, then other people will be happy by using the products as well. As more people purchase the items, they increase in popularity. So more

20 people jump on the bandwagon and buy certain products.

A third marketing method is called **reciprocity**. If someone gives a person something, that person wants to provide another thing in return. For instance, waiters at restaurants may give

25 diners mints along with their bills.

Studies have shown that customers leave bigger tips for waiters who give candy than those who do not.

Yet another marketing **ploy** is to create scarcity and urgency. To do this, stores sell a limited number of products or sell them for a short period of time. For instance, stores may have one-day sales. They often result in people **flocking** to them out of fear they will miss out on special deals.

All of these marketing techniques have been proven to work on consumers. Good marketing psychology relies on a number of them to attract more consumers. Words 350

P5 The marketing ploy of creating _____ and
30 urgency

Websites often rely on scarcity and urgency when selling goods to the public. Airlines might mention that only a few seats are available at a low price. Likewise, hotels may advertise that only one or two rooms are left for a discounted price.

💡 **Check what the passage is mainly about.**

a. Various marketing methods people are using nowadays

b. The reasons that psychologists are interested in marketing

c. A short history of marketing from the past to the present

d. The best way to market goods and services for restaurants and stores

Reading Comprehension

1   In paragraph 1, all of the following questions are answered EXCEPT:

   a. What is a definition of marketing?

   b. Why do some businesses use marketing psychology?

   c. How much can marketing improve a business's profits?

   d. How do many businesses advertise their products?

2   The word them in the passage refers to

   a. the cash registers

   b. people waiting in line

   c. these items

   d. their shopping carts

3   What does the underlined part in the passage mean?

   a. become happy

   b. like colorful images

   c. use public transportation

   d. act like other people

4   According to paragraph 4, which of the following is true about reciprocity?

   a. People use it to create a sense of urgency.

   b. It is the most successful marketing ploy.

   c. It uses the idea in psychology that people want to get what others have.

   d. Businesses use it to get something in return for what they give to customers.

5   The word scarcity in the passage is closest in meaning to

   a. shortage   b. price   c. popularity   d. appearance

6   According to paragraph 2, what do psychologists know about how consumers act?

   Psychologists know that _____ .

7   How do some stores create scarcity and urgency?

   _____

34

Organizing the Passage

Complete the organizer with the phrases in the box.

Marketing Psychology

Impulsive Shoppers	• Shoppers often make purchases ❶_____. • Supermarkets put goods ❷_____ because people waiting in line are likely to buy them.
The Bandwagon Effect	• Ads use colorful images and show happy people using products. • When more people buy certain items, ❸_____, so people jump on the bandwagon and buy them.
Reciprocity	• When a person gives another person something, the receiver wants to give something in return. • Waiters may give diners mints with their bills so that the diners then give them ❹_____.
Scarcity and Urgency	• Stores sell ❺_____ or sell them for a short period of time. • Stores have ❻_____ to get shoppers to flock to them to make purchases.

bigger tips	near cash registers	without thinking
one-day sales	their popularity increases	limited numbers of items

Summarizing the Passage

The first sentence of a short summary is provided below. Complete the summary by choosing THREE answer choices that express the most important ideas.

Marketing psychology enables businesses to sell more goods and services to consumers.

1 Sales are used to create feelings of scarcity and urgency to get shoppers to visit stores.

2 Psychologists have come up with many ways to get consumers to make purchases at stores.

3 Stores may place items near cash registers because impulsive shoppers are likely to buy them.

4 Waiters ask for big tips from diners and give mints to the ones that give them lots of money.

5 The bandwagon effect is used to convince large numbers of people to buy goods like others are doing.

Chapter 3
Health Science

Health science refers to the study of human health, diseases, illnesses, and other ailments that affect people. Health scientists and medical researchers try to determine the causes of various health and medical problems. They then search for treatments and ways to cure these problems or to keep people from getting them.

Health Science

Unit 5
Influenza

Think about the Topic

1 What are some symptoms of influenza?

2 What do you usually do if you have influenza?

Vocabulary Preview

A **Match the words with their definitions by writing the correct letters in the blanks.**

1 virus _____   a. a pig

2 outbreak _____   b. to start

3 pandemic _____   c. a death rate

4 subtype _____   d. relating to birds

5 combination _____   e. a special kind of something

6 originate _____   f. the sudden widespread start of a sickness

7 swine _____   g. a number of things brought together as one

8 avian _____   h. the rate at which something does its purpose

9 mortality rate _____   i. a very small living thing that can cause various diseases

10 effectiveness _____   j. a disease that affects an entire country, continent, or world

B **Choose the words that have similar** (*sim.*) **or opposite** (*opp.*) **meanings from the box.**

severe	worldwide	unite

1 mild _____ *opp.*

2 combine _____ *sim.*

3 global _____ *sim.*

Background Knowledge

There are many kinds of viruses. Some, such as smallpox, are extremely dangerous and once killed huge numbers of people. Others, like chickenpox and measles, can be harmful but usually do not result in death. Influenza is another virus. Better known as the flu, countless people get sick from it every year, and a surprisingly large number of people die from it, too.

Influenza

Q

What is each paragraph mainly about?

P2 How the _____ flu affects people in the United States

P3 The (causes / characteristics) of the influenza A, B, and C viruses

P4 The _____ of the influenza A virus

P5 Flu viruses from (animals / people) such as swine flu and avian flu

One of the most common illnesses people catch is influenza, frequently called the flu. A **virus** always causes it, and there are several which can sicken people.

The type of flu most people catch is called the seasonal flu because it
5 only appears at certain times. For instance, in the United States, it normally occurs during winter. For the most part, it sickens people between October and April. In the United States, anywhere between 140,000 and 960,000 people get hospitalized every flu season, and it kills 12,000 to 78,000 people each year.

10 Three viruses—called the influenza A, B, and C viruses—are the causes of seasonal flu. The A and B viruses are the most common. The A virus is the most serious form, being capable of causing major **outbreaks** called **pandemics**. The B virus is also harmful yet is less dangerous than the A virus. The C virus causes a milder sickness and is the least common.

15 The A virus additionally has several **subtypes**. These are called the H and N types and have names such as H3N2. The names are based on certain proteins which attach themselves to
20 the influenza viruses and then create new forms of influenza. There are a

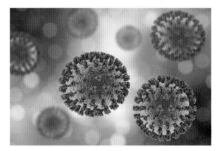

▲ Influenza viruses

total of sixteen H proteins and nine N proteins, which can combine to make numerous **combinations** of viruses.

There are also serious flu viruses which **originated** in animals. **Swine** flu,
25 for instance, is a combination of human, swine, and bird flu viruses. Known

as the H1N1 virus, it caused a pandemic that began in 2009 and ended the following year. During that time, it sickened numerous people and may have killed up to 200,000 people worldwide. The H5N1 virus, or **avian** flu, passes from birds to humans. It has a high **mortality rate**, and experts fear it could someday cause a global pandemic that kills millions of people.   *30*

While there are vaccines for influenza, they are of limited **effectiveness**. For that reason, people will continue to get sick and die from the flu.

Words 337

i Swine flu and avian flu have killed large numbers of humans in recent years. Variations of swine flu have also killed tens of millions of pigs. In 2019, China lost at least two hundred million pigs due to African swine flu. That number is roughly one-third of its pig population.

 Check what the passage is mainly about.

a. The most dangerous types of human and animal influenzas

b. The best ways for people with influenza to become healthy

c. Different types of influenza and how they affect people

d. Recent developments in the treatment of various influenzas

Reading Comprehension

1 In paragraph 2, which of the following is NOT mentioned about seasonal flu?

    a. Why many people in the United States get it

    b. When people in the United States mostly get it

    c. How many people in the United States die from it

    d. How many people in the United States stay in the hospital due to it

2 Why does the author mention The C virus?

    a. To blame it for causing some pandemics

    b. To compare it with other forms of influenza

    c. To argue that it is more dangerous than the B virus

    d. To claim it is the most common of the A, B, and C viruses

3 Which of the following is true about the influenza A virus?

    a. There are sixteen N proteins which can attach to it.

    b. Some of its subtypes have killed millions of people.

    c. The names of its subtypes are based on how many viruses they have.

    d. New forms of influenza are created by H proteins and N proteins.

4 The word it in the passage refers to

    a. the H1N1 virus   b. a pandemic

    c. the H5N1 virus   d. a high mortality rate

5 In paragraph 5, which of the following can be inferred about the H5N1 virus?

    a. It may become a highly deadly virus.

    b. It affects humans, birds, and pigs.

    c. It was just discovered in recent years.

    d. It makes millions of people sick each year.

6 What is the influenza A virus?

    It is the most _____.

7 When does the seasonal flu usually sicken people?

    _____

Organizing the Passage

Complete the organizer with the phrases in the box.

Influenza	
Seasonal Flu	• It appears in winter in the United States. • It ❶_____ between 140,000 and 960,000 people and kill 12,000 to 78,000 people in the U.S. annually. • The A, B, and C viruses are the causes of it.
The Features of the A, B, and C Viruses	• The A virus can cause pandemics. • The B virus is harmful but ❷_____ than the A virus. • The C virus causes a mild form of the flu and is the least common one.
The Subtypes of the A Virus	• The A virus has several subtypes that contain ❸_____ and N proteins. • They attach themselves to the virus and ❹_____ of influenza.
Animal Viruses	• Swine flu is a combination of ❺_____ flu viruses. • Avian flu passes from birds to humans and has a ❻_____.

high mortality rate	can hospitalize	create new forms
less dangerous	human, swine, and bird	H proteins

Summarizing the Passage

Use the phrases in the box to complete the summary.

can cause pandemics		has several subtypes
a common illness	swine flu	tens of thousands

Influenza is ❶_____ many people catch. In the United States, people get seasonal flu in winter. It hospitalizes hundreds of thousands of people and kills ❷_____ of people annually. The influenza A, B, and C viruses cause seasonal flu. The A virus is serious and ❸_____. The B and C viruses are less dangerous. The A virus ❹_____ because H proteins and N proteins can make new forms of influenza. ❺_____ has sickened and killed large numbers of people. And avian flu has a high mortality rate.

Unit 6

Nanotechnology and Medical Science

Think about the Topic

1 What is nanotechnology?

2 What health or medical benefits do you think nanotechnology can provide?

Vocabulary Preview

A   **Match the words with their definitions by writing the correct letters in the blanks.**

1 atom _____ a. a very early stage

2 building block _____ b. to force a fluid into a body

3 bloodstream _____ c. to cure; to make healthy

4 monitor _____ d. a basic component of something

5 cell _____ e. to watch over or observe closely

6 inject _____ f. the smallest compound of an element

7 heal _____ g. the basic structural unit of all organisms

8 surgery _____ h. the blood that flows through the body

9 invasive _____ i. referring to cutting into a person's body

10 infancy _____ j. the act of cutting into a person to improve a part of that individual's body

B   **Choose the words that have similar** (*sim.*) **or opposite** (*opp.*) **meanings from the box.**

assault	area	injure

1 field _____ *sim.*

2 heal _____ *opp.*

3 attack _____ *sim.*

Background Knowledge

Thanks to modern technology, scientists and researchers have been able to cure many diseases. They have also been able to make surgery less dangerous and invasive for patients. One day, they may be able to eliminate the need for surgery that cuts people open. They may also be able to cure almost any disease. The key to these is nanotechnology.

Nanotechnology and Medical Science

Q

What is each paragraph mainly about?

P1 (Where / What) nanotechnology is

P2 How nanorobots will help various _____

P3 The process through which nanorobots will be used to heal (patients / bloodstream)

P4 How nanorobots will fight _____ and conduct surgery

Nanotechnology involves the controlling of matter at a very small level. Its name comes from the unit of measurement called a nanometer. It is one billionth of a meter in size. This is smaller than the width of a human hair. Yet it is larger than a single **atom**.

5 Scientists want to use nanotechnology to create very light yet strong **building blocks**. These will then be used to build tiny machines called nanorobots. At present, scientists in many fields are working on this technology. They believe it will be helpful to the construction, textile, transportation, and food safety industries.

10 They also expect it to be useful to the field of medicine. For instance, some scientists hope to create nanorobots able to carry both a camera and medicine. Patients will drink a liquid with thousands or even millions of these nanorobots. They will enter the **bloodstream**. Then, they will move to problem areas. Doctors will **monitor** the entire process thanks to 15 the _____ in each nanorobot. Upon finding cancer **cells**, the doctors will order the nanorobots to **inject** medicine into those places. It will then work quickly to **heal** the patient.

This will provide patients with many benefits. First of all, most cancer treatments today require procedures that attack all cells—both healthy and 20 unhealthy ones. This results in healthy cells being killed. But nanorobots will lessen the damage to the body by only attacking cancer cells. They will also conduct **surgery** deep inside the body. 25 As a result, doctors will no longer have to

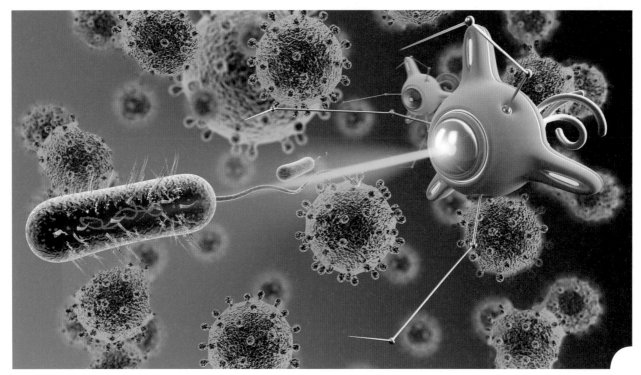

▲ A nanorobot

cut into patients' bodies. This will reduce the risk of **invasive** surgeries. It will also result in shorter recovery times for patients.

❶ At present, medical nanotechnology is in its **infancy**. ❷ So nanorobots able to perform medical treatments do not exist yet. ❸ In a few years, it is likely that they will be used to cure cancer and other diseases and to make surgery simple and painless. ❹ Words 332

🔲 What scientists hope to do with _____ in a few years

30

> *i* One problem with nanorobots is that scientists must make them small enough to be able to move through the body. But they must also be able to carry medicine or tools. Then, they must be able to leave the body at some point.

 Check what the passage is mainly about.

a. The problems researchers have with developing nanorobots

b. Which advances scientists have made in the field of nanotechnology

c. The ability of nanorobots to move through the body to help people

d. How nanotechnology can be used to help patients with various problems

Reading Comprehension

1. Which of the following is true about nanotechnology?
   a. It is already highly developed in the medical industry.
   b. It creates nanorobots that are smaller than an atom.
   c. It might be useful in many fields in the future.
   d. It is used by scientists to control matter right now.

2. What is the best choice for the blank?
   a. camera   b. medicine   c. needle   d. liquid

3. In paragraph 3, all of the following questions are answered EXCEPT:
   a. How will nanorobots enter a patient's body?
   b. How long will it take nanorobots to find problem areas?
   c. What will nanorobots do when they find cancer cells?
   d. What do scientists hope that some nanorobots will be able to carry?

4. Which of the following can be inferred about nanorobots according to paragraph 4?
   a. They may attack healthy cells.
   b. They will be harmful to some cancer patients.
   c. Patients will not feel good about surgeries using them.
   d. Surgeries with them will be safer than invasive surgeries.

5. Where would the following sentence best fit in paragraph 5?

However, scientists and engineers are working hand in hand to develop nanorobots.

   a. ❶   b. ❷   c. ❸   d. ❹

6. How small is a nanometer?
   It is smaller than _____ .

7. According to paragraph 4, how will nanorobots help patients with cancer?

   _____

Organizing the Passage

Complete the organizer with the phrases in the box.

Nanotechnology and Medical Science

Nanotechnology	• It controls matter at a very small level. • Its name comes from nanometer, which is one billionth of a meter in size. • Scientists will use it to create very light yet ❶_____ that can make nanorobots.
Nanorobots in the Field of Medicine	• They will be useful in the field of medicine because they will carry a camera and medicine. • They will ❷_____ and then move to problem areas. • Then, doctors can monitor the process as the nanorobots ❸_____.
Benefits of Nanotechnology	• Nanorobots will only ❹_____, so they will lessen the damage to the body. • They will ❺_____ deep in the body, so doctors will not have to cut into patients' bodies. • Patients will have ❻_____ thanks to nanotechnology.

strong building blocks   attack cancer cells   shorter recovery times
conduct surgery   enter the bloodstream   inject medicine

Summarizing the Passage

The first sentence of a short summary is provided below. Complete the summary by choosing THREE answer choices that express the most important ideas.

Scientists hope to use nanotechnology to provide medical treatment for people in the future.

1 Nanorobots will carry a camera and medicine to help doctors see where the problem area is.

2 Scientists have not yet done much with nanotechnology because the technology is very advanced.

3 Scientists plan to introduce machines called nanorobots into the body to provide medical care.

4 A nanometer is something so small that it is not even as wide as a single human hair.

5 It may be possible to use nanotechnology to provide care for cancer patients and to conduct noninvasive surgeries.

Chapter 4

Zoology

Zoology refers to the study of animals and the ecosystems they live in. Zoologists often focus on learning about the physical characteristics of animals as well as how they interact with the other animals they live with. They try to understand how animals survive and what makes them thrive or go extinct.

Unit 7

The Extinction of Prehistoric Megafauna

A shaggy dire wolf

Think about the Topic

1 What are some examples of megafauna?

2 What do you think caused some megafauna to go extinct in the past?

Vocabulary Preview

A **Match the words with their definitions by writing the correct letters in the blanks.**

1 prehistoric _____ a. to appear

2 vanish _____ b. an idea about something

3 theory _____ c. to disappear entirely

4 overhunting _____ d. protection against attack

5 settlement _____ e. to do better than another in a contest

6 speculate _____ f. to think about and to make a guess

7 emerge _____ g. existing in the time before recorded history

8 defense _____ h. the act of killing too many animals in a certain area

9 population explosion _____ i. a place where people move to and build homes

10 outcompete _____ j. a sudden increase in the number of people, animals, or other organisms in an area

B **Choose the words that have similar (*sim.*) or opposite (*opp.*) meanings from the box.**

suggest   abandon   living

1 extinct _____ *opp.*

2 propose _____ *sim.*

3 settle _____ *opp.*

Background Knowledge

Megafauna have lived on the Earth for millions of years. They are typically considered animals that weigh at least 200 kilograms. There are megafauna such as elephants, hippos, whales, and sharks today. In the past, many dinosaurs were megafauna. Other animals, including the woolly mammoth, the dire wolf, and the giant sloth, were also megafauna, but they all went extinct.

The Extinction of Prehistoric Megafauna

Q

What is each paragraph mainly about?

P1 Which megafauna lived during (prehistoric / modern) times

P2 What happened to many megafauna living in _____

P3 A theory about how (the climate / humans) contributed to the extinction of megafauna

P4 A theory on how _____ and the changing climate affected megafauna

During **prehistoric** times, there were large numbers of megafauna. These were animals that were very large and heavy. They were especially big in comparison to animals alive now. Two examples were the woolly mammoth and the saber-toothed tiger. There were also huge versions
5 of modern animals. Among them were sloths, deer, bears, wolves, and horses.

Many of these animals lived in North America. Yet they started going extinct around 60,000 years ago. Then, they **vanished** completely by 9,000 B.C. This happened right around the end of the last major ice age.
10 Nobody is sure exactly how or why these animals went extinct. But several **theories** have been proposed.

Overhunting by humans was likely a major cause of the extinction of these animals in North America. North America was once empty of human **settlements**. But during the last ice age, sea levels were lower.
15 This let a land bridge between Asia and North America form. Humans crossed this bridge and settled both North America and South America. As they spread, they
20 hunted animals. In a fairly short period of time, they managed to wipe out most megafauna around 11,000 years ago.

▲ A saber-toothed tiger

Some megafauna had already gone extinct by the time humans reached
25 North America though. So scientists **speculate** that diseases were responsible for killing them. As the weather got warmer, new diseases

▲ A group of woolly mammoths

may have **emerged**. The animals would have had no **defenses** against them. The changing climate itself may have killed many animals, too. When the ice age ended and warm weather began, there was a **population explosion** of many species. These animals may have **outcompeted** megafauna for food sources. In the struggle for survival, <u>some species were not strong enough to succeed</u>.

30

In all likelihood, it was a combination of all three theories that caused the woolly mammoth and other large animals to go extinct. Until more fossils are dug up and more research on the planet done, the real reason—or reasons—will remain a mystery to scientists.   Words 329

35

i Some megafauna went extinct at different times in various places. For instance, the woolly mammoth went extinct in Europe much earlier than it did in North America and parts of Asia. Some managed to survive on Wrangel Island in Russia until around 1600 B.C.

 Check what the passage is mainly about.

 a. The relationship between humans and megafauna

 b. Different types of megafauna that once lived in North America

 c. The reasons that various large animals died out in the past

 d. The manner in which diseases killed great numbers of large animals

Reading Comprehension

1 Why does the author mention the woolly mammoth and the saber-toothed tiger?

   a. To compare them with other megafauna
   b. To cite them as the most famous megafauna
   c. To name them as two kinds of prehistoric megafauna
   d. To argue they were bigger than other prehistoric megafauna

2 According to paragraph 2, which of the following is true about megafauna in North America?

   a. They went extinct all of a sudden.
   b. It is not known exactly why they all died out.
   c. Most of them died before the ice age began.
   d. Nobody knows which ones lived there.

3 The phrase wipe out in the passage is closest in meaning to

   a. hide   b. migrate   c. change   d. kill

4 What does the underlined part in the passage mean?

   a. some animals evolved a lot
   b. some animals killed other animals
   c. some animals went extinct
   d. some animals moved to other places

5 In paragraph 4, all of the following questions are answered EXCEPT:

   a. What happened when the weather became warmer in the past?
   b. Why did the new diseases kill lots of animals?
   c. When was there a population explosion of many species?
   d. Which megafauna went extinct before humans arrived in North America?

6 What are megafauna?

   They are animals that are _____.

7 What is the importance of the land bridge between Asia and North America in the past?

   _____

Organizing the Passage

Complete the organizer with the phrases in the box.

The Extinction of Prehistoric Megafauna	
North American Megafauna	• Many of these animals ❶_____ between around 60,000 years ago and 9,000 B.C. • The final extinctions happened around the end of the ❷_____.
Reasons for Extinction	• Hunting by humans that crossed ❸_____ between Asia and North America killed many megafauna. • ❹_____ may have killed megafauna when the weather became warmer. • Other animals had ❺_____ when the ice age ended. • They ❻_____ for food, so the megafauna went extinct.

a population explosion	went extinct	the land bridge
outcompeted megafauna	some diseases	last major ice age

Summarizing the Passage

The first sentence of a short summary is provided below. Complete the summary by choosing THREE answer choices that express the most important ideas.

Prehistoric megafauna living in North America went extinct for various reasons.

1 Humans entered North and South America by a land bridge and killed many megafauna.

2 The ice age was a time when enough food was hard to find for a big number of very large animals.

3 Some diseases may have appeared as the weather got warmer and killed defenseless megafauna.

4 Woolly mammoths and saber-toothed tigers were some of the megafauna that went extinct in the past.

5 A population explosion of species after the ice age ended resulted in animals outcompeting megafauna for food.

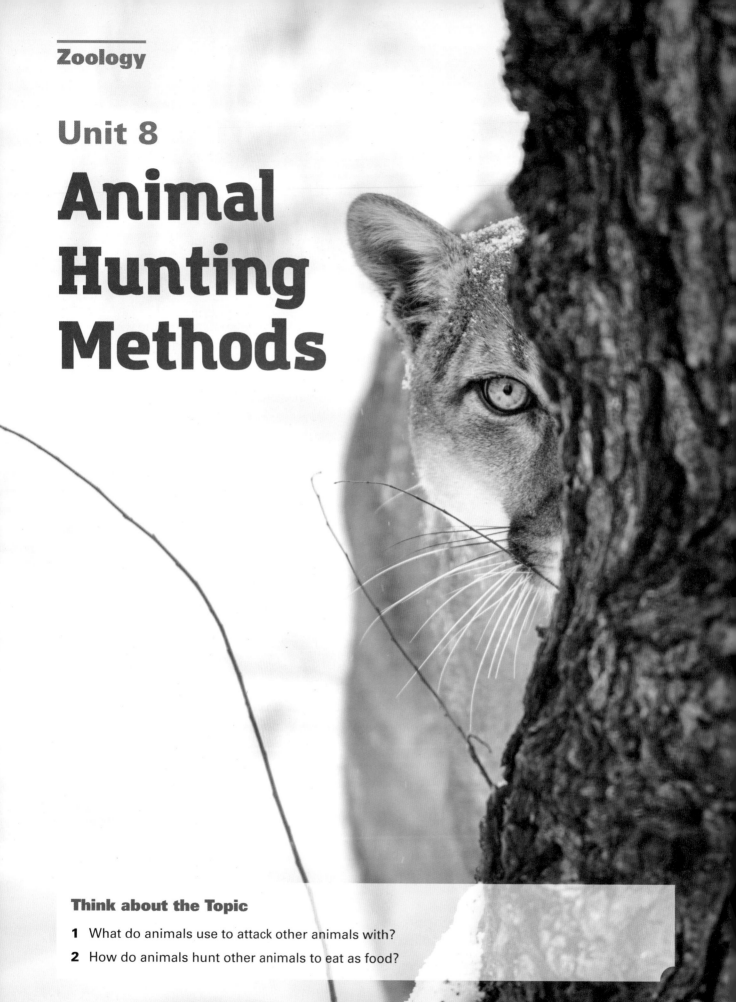

Unit 8
Animal Hunting Methods

Think about the Topic

1 What do animals use to attack other animals with?

2 How do animals hunt other animals to eat as food?

Vocabulary Preview

A **Match the words with their definitions by writing the correct letters in the blanks.**

1 ambush _____ a. quietly and hidden

2 stalk _____ b. afterward; next

3 stealthily _____ c. to eat, often completely

4 lunge _____ d. a group of animals, often predators

5 consume _____ e. to run after or chase to catch something

6 pack _____ f. suddenly to move quickly toward something

7 creep _____ g. to attack an animal from a hidden position

8 pursue _____ h. to follow prey slowly and quietly to catch it

9 paralyze _____ i. to move slowly with one's body close to the ground

10 subsequently _____ j. to cause to be unable to move, such as by using poison

B **Choose the words that have similar** (*sim.*) **or opposite** (*opp.*) **meanings from the box.**

separately	use	insert

1 employ _____ *sim.*

2 jointly _____ *opp.*

3 inject _____ *sim.*

Background Knowledge

Some animals eat plants, but other animals consume animals. These animals, called predators, must hunt prey and catch it to kill and eat it. Animals have developed many ways to hunt others. Predators typically have sharp teeth and claws. They may be able to run fast or can hide well so that other animals cannot see them. These enable animals to capture prey, which lets them survive.

Animal Hunting Methods

Q

What is each paragraph mainly about?

P2 Which animals are

hunters and how they kill prey

P3 (How / Why) some animals use group attacks to kill prey

P4 The manner in which some animals (creep / stalk) and chase prey

When predators hunt other animals, called prey, they utilize several methods of attack. The four most common are to **ambush** prey, to attack in groups, to **stalk** and chase prey, and to employ poison or venom.

Ambush hunters must find a place to lie in wait for an animal to approach
5 their position. Tigers, chameleons, and numerous snakes are ambush hunters. Another common ambush hunter is the crocodile. ❶ When an animal goes down to the edge of the water to drink, the crocodile **stealthily** moves closer. ❷ Suddenly, it **lunges**, grabs its prey, drags it into the water, and drowns it. ❸ Once dead, the animal can be **consumed** by the
10 crocodile. ❹

The group attack is an effective method utilized by social animals such as lions and wolves. Wolves, for instance, hunt in **packs**. When they find a large animal such as a deer, elk, or moose, they surround it. They bite at its legs to attempt to slow it down and then jointly move in for the kill. Orcas—
15 killer whales—also form groups to attack whales and seals. They chase their prey to tire it out. Then, when it becomes weak, the orcas bite and kill their target.

Stalking and chasing prey is the preferred hunting method of many big cats. They stalk their prey by **creeping** as close as possible to it. Then, they

▾ A cheetah chasing its prey

lunge toward it and begin chasing the animal. Cheetahs, the fastest land 20
animals, utilize this method but are not always successful because the prey
they **pursue** can also run swiftly.

Large numbers of insects and reptiles use poison or venom when hunting.
They bite their prey and inject poison or venom into its body. As the poison
takes effect, the animal weakens, slows down, and becomes **paralyzed**. 25
The predator can **subsequently** drag the dead animal's body away or eat it
on the spot.

P5 How poison and
_____ can
help animals hunt

These are the four primary methods predators use. While they are not
always successful, they enable predators to feed enough to survive.

Words 345

 Check what the passage is mainly about.

   a. The manner in which animals evolved to develop hunting methods
   b. The four primary methods that animals use to hunt others
   c. The way that zoologists believe is the best for animals to hunt
   d. The battles between predators and prey that may take place

i Prey animals have many
defenses they can use
to keep from being killed
by predators. Some have
great speed while others
can hide well. They may
also have horns or antlers
which they can use to fight
predators if they need to.

Reading Comprehension

1 Where would the following sentence best fit in paragraph 2?

> It typically waits in water nearby shore while keeping only its eyes above the water.

a. ❶   b. ❷   c. ❸   d. ❹

2 The word it in the passage refers to

a. the edge of the water
c. its prey

b. the crocodile
d. the water

3 According to paragraph 3, which of the following is NOT mentioned about group attacks?

a. What kinds of animals use that method
b. Which animals are hunted by wolf packs
c. How predators move to kill their prey
d. How animals defend themselves from predators

4 In paragraph 4, which of the following can be inferred about cheetahs?

a. They prefer to hunt in large groups of animals.
b. They are not always fast enough to catch animals.
c. They usually hunt animals that are bigger than they are.
d. Their hunting method is more successful than other ones.

5 According to paragraph 5, which of the following is true about animals that use poison or venom?

a. They are much smaller than the animals which they attack.
b. They almost always instantly kill their prey after biting it.
c. Prey animals attacked by them can sometimes run away successfully.
d. Reptiles and insects are known to frequently use this method.

6 Which hunting method do many big cats use?

The preferred hunting method of many big cats is _____.

7 How do orcas hunt their prey in groups?

_____

Organizing the Passage

Complete the organizer with the phrases in the box.

Animal Hunting Methods	
Ambush Hunters	• Tigers, chameleons, snakes, and crocodiles are ambush hunters. • They ❶＿＿＿＿＿＿＿ for an animal to approach their position and then attack it.
Group Attack	• Social animals such as ❷＿＿＿＿＿＿＿ use this method. • Wolves attack large animals like deer, elk, and moose together. • Orcas hunt whales and seals together ❸＿＿＿＿＿＿＿.
Stalk and Chase	• This method is often used ❹＿＿＿＿＿＿＿. • Animals like the cheetah ❺＿＿＿＿＿＿＿ to their prey and chase it.
Poison or Venom	• Insects and reptiles may use this method to hunt with. • They inject poison or venom into the body of their prey, and then they wait for the animal ❻＿＿＿＿＿＿＿.

in groups	to be paralyzed	lie in wait
lions and wolves	creep close	by big cats

Summarizing the Passage

Use the phrases in the box to complete the summary.

their great speed	approach their position
use group attacks	poison or venom	stalk and chase

Predators have several methods to kill prey. Ambush hunters wait for animals to
❶＿＿＿＿＿＿＿ and then attack it. Tigers, chameleons, snakes, and crocodiles use this
method. Social animals such as wolves and orcas ❷＿＿＿＿＿＿＿. They work together to
attack and kill animals. Big cats prefer to ❸＿＿＿＿＿＿＿ their prey. Cheetahs may use
❹＿＿＿＿＿＿＿ to run after animals. Insects and reptiles may use ❺＿＿＿＿＿＿＿.
It is injected into the body of a prey animal, which gets paralyzed and can then be eaten.

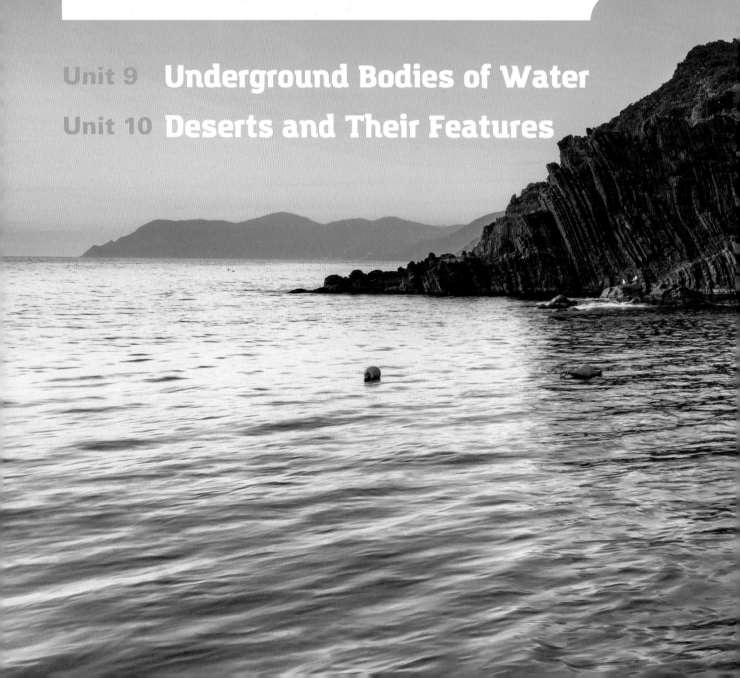

Chapter 5
Geography

Geography refers to the study of the land, oceans, and features of the Earth. Geographers not only study the land but also focus on its relationship with humans and the environment. Geographers attempt to understand the complexities of the Earth and the people living on it.

Unit 9

Underground Bodies of Water

Think about the Topic

1   What kinds of bodies of water are underground?

2   How do you think large amounts of water get underground?

Vocabulary Preview

A **Match the words with their definitions by writing the correct letters in the blanks.**

1 body _____ a. to end up

2 seep _____ b. over time; finally

3 eventually _____ c. a large mass of something

4 wind up _____ d. the beginning of something

5 temporary _____ e. to gradually destroy something over time

6 acre _____ f. an area of land covering 4,047 square meters

7 erode _____ g. to pass or flow slowly through a substance

8 channel _____ h. lasting for a certain period of time; not permanent

9 crust _____ i. the bottom of a waterway such as a stream or river

10 origin _____ j. the surface of the Earth and the part directly beneath it

B **Choose the words that have similar** (*sim.*) **or opposite** (*opp.*) **meanings from the box.**

investigate	descend	beforehand

1 rise _____ *opp.*

2 explore _____ *sim.*

3 previously _____ *sim.*

Background Knowledge

There are places in deserts where water can be found. These are called oases, and they come from underground sources of water that rise to the surface. As people have begun investigating the land beneath the Earth's surface, they have discovered that underground bodies of water are not rare. In fact, they exist in many places around the Earth.

Underground Bodies of Water

Q

What is each paragraph mainly about?

P1 Where on the Earth there are bodies of

_____

P2 How underground lakes (flow / form)

More than seventy percent of the Earth's surface is covered by its oceans. Other large areas of land are covered by seas, lakes, and rivers. These are not the only places where there is water though. There are also lakes, rivers, and oceans beneath the Earth's surface.

5 Lakes are the most common **bodies** of water underground. Many of them are found in cave systems. Normally, they form when water on the surface **seeps** into
10 the ground, where it **eventually winds up** in a cave. The levels of many underground lakes rise and

▲ An underground lake called Martel

fall throughout the year. **Temporary** lakes form during the rainy season and can be dangerous to people who are exploring caves. The world's biggest
15 underground lake is in Dragon's Breath Cave in Namibia, a country in Africa. It covers an area of around five **acres**.

P3 What kinds of underground

_____ there are and how they flow

There are some rivers that flow underground, too. Some are _____, like the Fleet River in London, England, and the Neglinnaya River in Moscow, Russia. Others are naturally flowing rivers.
20 They usually move through cave systems. In other cases, water may **erode** limestone or other soft rocks underground and then travel through the **channels** it creates. These rivers may be entirely underwater or may rise to the surface at some places. Many rivers have their own ecosystems full of fish and plants.

P4 An underground ocean that has been (discovered / explored)

25 Scientists have also discovered that there is a huge ocean lying deep beneath the Earth's surface. It is located under part of eastern North

▲ An underground river

America, and is roughly 660 kilometers beneath the Earth's **crust**. It is possible that this ocean contains three times more water than all of the Earth's oceans combined. The existence of this ocean has led scientists to believe that the Earth's water may have its **origins** on the planet. *30* Previously, many had speculated that the planet's water arrived when *comets impacted the surface.

It is likely that many more underground lakes, rivers, and oceans exist, but people are not aware of them. In the future, more of them will be discovered as advances in technology make finding them easier. Words 342

*comet: a mass of ice, dust, and gas that moves around the sun and often develops a long tail when it gets near the sun

 Check the main idea of the passage.

    a. The majority of the Earth's surface is covered by bodies of water.

    b. There are all kinds of bodies of water beneath the Earth's surface.

    c. An underground ocean is the largest body of water on the entire planet.

    d. Some underground rivers are natural while others are made by people.

i Some scientists believe that the Earth's water comes from comets. They claim that millions or billions of years ago, comets impacted the Earth. The water that they carried was then distributed throughout the Earth and formed its oceans, rivers, and lakes.

Reading Comprehension

1 According to paragraph 2, which of the following is NOT true about underground lakes?

   a. Some of them may form during a specific season.

   b. They are less common than underground rivers.

   c. The largest one on the Earth covers around five acres.

   d. They form from water seeping down into caves.

2 What is the best choice for the blank?

   a. long   b. aboveground   c. manmade   d. discovered

3 In paragraph 3, which of the following is mentioned about underground rivers?

   a. Where underground they often flow

   b. How long it takes for them to form

   c. How many of them there are on the Earth

   d. What kinds of fish and plants may live in them

4 In paragraph 4, which of the following can be inferred about the underground ocean?

   a. It was discovered hundreds of years ago.

   b. Scientists know exactly when it was formed.

   c. It is larger than all of the Earth's oceans.

   d. Comets provided the water found in it.

5 The word impacted in the passage is closest in meaning to

   a. approached   b. eroded   c. changed   d. hit

6 Where is the world's biggest underground lake?

The world's biggest underground lake is in _____.

7 Where is the underground ocean located?

_____

70

Organizing the Passage

Select the appropriate statements from the answer choices and match them to the underground body of water to which they relate. Two of the answer choices will NOT be used.

Lake	River	Ocean
•	•	•
•	•	•
	•	

1. Can be found beneath part of North America
2. Can flow for more than 1,000 kilometers
3. Is a big one that can be found in Africa
4. Can be natural or be made by people
5. Is found hundreds of kilometers beneath the Earth's surface
6. Is one located under both London and Moscow
7. Is used by people to provide them with fresh water
8. May form when flowing water erodes limestone
9. May be dangerous to people when it temporarily forms

Summarizing the Passage

Use the phrases in the box to complete the summary.

rise to the surface	three times more
the rainy season in cave systems	through channels

There are not only bodies of water on the Earth's surface but also beneath it. Lakes are the most common underground bodies of water and often form ❶_____. They can rise and fall. And temporary ones may be dangerous to people during ❷_____. There are both manmade and natural underground rivers. They flow through cave systems or ❸_____ they create. Some are entirely underwater whereas others may ❹_____. There is an enormous ocean beneath North America. It may have ❺_____ water than all of the oceans on the surface combined.

Unit 10
Deserts and Their Features

Vocabulary Preview

A **Match the words with their definitions by writing the correct letters in the blanks.**

1 precipitation _____ a. small stones

2 semiarid _____ b. earth; dirt

3 bush _____ c. widespread; very large

4 periodic _____ d. rain, snow, ice, etc. that falls from the sky

5 gravel _____ e. happening or appearing at regular intervals

6 cactus (*pl.* cacti) _____ f. receiving little rainfall throughout the year

7 soil _____ g. one of the seven large landmasses on the Earth

8 extensive _____ h. a plant that has small branches and is smaller than a tree

9 continent _____ i. a desert plant that has a tall, leafless stem with sharp points

10 landform _____ j. a certain feature of the Earth's surface, such as a mountain, plain, or valley

B **Choose the words that have similar (*sim.*) or opposite (*opp.*) meanings from the box.**

acquire	different	irregular

1 distinct _____ *sim.*

2 periodic _____ *opp.*

3 obtain _____ *sim.*

Background Knowledge

There are all kinds of ecosystems on the Earth. On land, forests, grasslands, plains, and taiga are four common ecosystems. Deserts are another common ecosystem and are found on every continent on the Earth. There are many types of deserts, so some have features that are different from others.

Deserts and Their Features

Deserts are among the most common ecosystems as they cover approximately twenty percent of the Earth's land surface. ❶ All deserts share one feature: They receive a small amount of annual **precipitation**. ❷ At most, they receive fifty centimeters of precipitation a year. ❸ There are
5 four main types of deserts: subtropical, **semiarid**, coastal, and polar, and each has its own distinct characteristics. ❹

When most people think of deserts, subtropical, or hot-and-dry, deserts come to mind. They are covered with sand and have few plants, mostly small **bushes** and short trees. They are hot all year and undergo
10 temperature shifts of up to forty-five degrees Celsius between day and night. The Sahara Desert in Africa and the Arabian Desert in the Middle East are subtropical deserts.

Semiarid deserts are also called cold winter deserts. They get long, dry summers and winters with **periodic** rainfall. They are not as hot as
15 subtropical deserts and can be cold during winter. Some have sand whereas others have **gravel** or rocks on their surfaces. **Cacti** are common in these deserts. The Great Basin Desert in the United States is a semiarid desert.

20 Coastal deserts are located along the shores of oceans. They have cool to warm weather. Summers are long and warm while winters are cold. Their **soil** tends to have a high salt content, so their plants normally have **extensive** root systems. This allows
25 the plants to obtain nutrients from deep within the soil. The Atacama Desert in South America is a

▲ The Atacama Desert

coastal desert and one of the Earth's driest places. Parts of it have received no rainfall in centuries.

The final type of desert is the polar desert. These include the **continent** of Antarctica and the northern Arctic Desert. While these areas are constantly covered with snow, they are considered deserts because they receive small amounts of precipitation annually. Most places in these deserts receive between fifteen and twenty-five centimeters of it each year.

30

P5 The characteristics of _____ deserts

Deserts are highly diverse **landforms**. While none receives much rain or snow, they vary in temperature, soil, and plant life. Words 347

 Check what the passage is mainly about.

    a. The quality of the soil in the world's deserts

    b. Types of deserts and what each of them is like

    c. The most famous deserts found on the Earth

    d. Precipitation amounts in deserts around the world

i Despite harsh conditions, all kinds of animals live in deserts. Reptiles, mammals, birds, insects, and fish all live in deserts. Many of these animals have adapted over time to get used to the lack of water in deserts.

Reading Comprehension

1 Where would the following sentence best fit in paragraph 1?

Most receive less than half that amount though.

   a. ❶   b. ❷   c. ❸   d. ❹

2 The word shifts in the passage is closest in meaning to

   a. changes   b. waves   c. increases   d. periods

3 According to paragraph 3, which of the following is true about semiarid deserts?

   a. They have few plants.
   b. They are dry all year around.
   c. They are all covered with gravel or rocks.
   d. Their temperatures differ in summer and winter.

4 In paragraph 4, all of the following questions are answered EXCEPT:

   a. Where are coastal deserts located?
   b. What does the soil in coastal deserts contain?
   c. Which desert is one of the driest in the world?
   d. How much rainfall do coastal deserts usually get in a year?

5 According to paragraph 5, why are polar deserts considered deserts?

   a. Because they are always covered with snow
   b. Because there are few plants living in them
   c. Because they get small amounts of precipitation in a year
   d. Because the temperatures are low all year round

6 What are two subtropical deserts?

   Two subtropical deserts are _____.

7 What is the role of the extensive root systems of plants in the coastal deserts?

   _____

Organizing the Passage

Complete the organizer with the phrases in the box.

	Deserts and Their Features
Subtropical Deserts	• They have ❶_____, and are hot all year. • The Sahara Desert in Africa and the Arabian Desert in the Middle East are subtropical deserts.
Semiarid Deserts	• They are ❷_____ as subtropical deserts. • They may have ❸_____ on their surfaces. • The Great Basin Desert in the United States is one of these deserts.
Coastal Deserts	• They are located near oceans and have ❹_____. • They ❺_____, so their plants have extensive root systems. • The Atacama Desert in South America is one of these deserts.
Polar Deserts	• Two of these deserts are Antarctica and the northern Arctic Desert. • They are ❻_____ all year but get little precipitation annually.

covered with snow	not as hot	cool to warm weather
sand and few plants	have salty soil	sand, gravel, or rocks

Summarizing the Passage

Use the phrases in the box to complete the summary.

the shores of oceans	get cold in winter	
annual precipitation	polar deserts	cacti growing

There are four main types of deserts, and all of them get a small amount of

❶_____. Subtropical deserts are hot and sandy. They include the Sahara Desert

and the Arabian Desert. Semiarid deserts get long, dry summers and can ❷_____.

They often have ❸_____ in them. Coastal deserts like the Atacama Desert

are found along ❹_____. They can have cold winters and have salty soil.

❺_____ like Antarctica and the northern Arctic Desert are covered with snow all

year and get small amounts of precipitation.

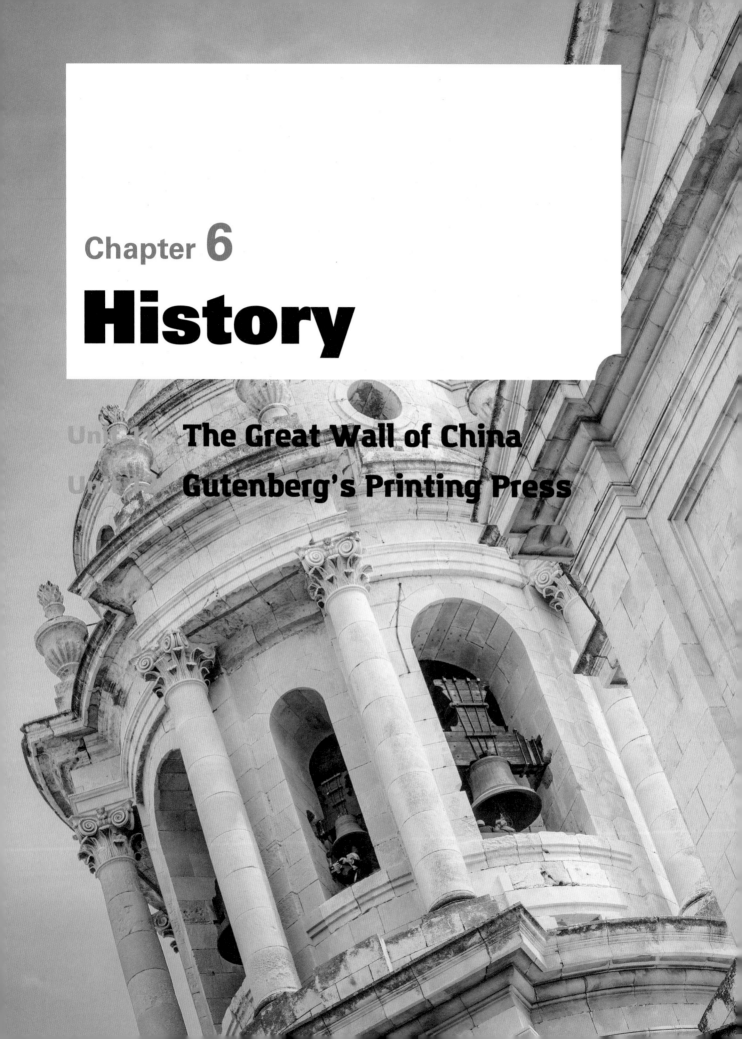

Chapter **6**

History

The Great Wall of China
Gutenberg's Printing Press

History refers to the study of the past. Historians study people and their actions in the past. They try to learn not only what happened in the past but why it happened and what made people act in certain ways.

Unit 11
The Great Wall of China

Think about the Topic

1 Why was the Great Wall of China built?

2 How long did it take to build the Great Wall of China?

Vocabulary Preview

A **Match the words with their definitions by writing the correct letters in the blanks.**

1 stretch   _____   a. to build

2 counter   _____   b. to extend

3 fortified   _____   c. to fight or oppose

4 straw   _____   d. a building to keep horses in

5 erect   _____   e. strengthened, often for defense

6 starvation   _____   f. a building in which soldiers live

7 watchtower   _____   g. the act of dying due to a lack of food

8 barracks   _____   h. the condition of being broken or in need of fixing

9 stable   _____   i. the dry stems of grain such as wheat, rye, or barley

10 disrepair   _____   j. a tall structure with guards looking for enemies

B **Choose the words that have similar** (*sim.*) **or opposite** (*opp.*) **meanings from the box.**

tiredness	destroy	guess

1 estimate   _____   *sim.*

2 exhaustion   _____   *sim.*

3 erect   _____   *opp.*

Background Knowledge

Humans have been fighting wars for thousands of years. In many cases, armies invade the land of another people and attack them. To try to stop them, people often build defenses. Some of the best defenses are walls. Sometimes people put walls around castles or cities. As for China, it built a wall extending thousands of kilometers.

The Great Wall of China

Q

What is each paragraph mainly about?

P2 How and why the Great Wall of China was _____ over time

P3 What construction _____ were used and how many people died building it

P4 What kinds of structures were built on and (near / away from) the wall

In northern China, a wall **stretches** from the sea in the east to land far in the west. While not connected everywhere, these walls are collectively known as the Great Wall of China. It has a history dating back thousands of years.

In the seventh century B.C., China
5 was not unified, and there were many tribes warring with one another. To **counter** their enemies, tribes began building walls. Later, between 226 and 200 B.C., Qin Shi Huang, China's
10 first emperor, ordered construction of a **fortified** wall. Following him, more construction work as well as renovations were done for centuries. Later, during the Ming Dynasty, which lasted from 1368 to 1644, more construction and repair work occurred. Altogether, more than 21,000 kilometers of wall were constructed. The walls themselves average around
15 six meters in width and can be up to fifteen meters high.

Much of the Great Wall was initially constructed with earth, **straw**, and tree branches while stones were added later. During the Ming Dynasty, bricks were the most common construction material. Nobody knows how many people were involved in **erecting** the wall, but experts estimate
20 that millions were involved in the process. Up to a million people may have died working on the wall because of accidents, exhaustion, disease, **starvation**, and animal attacks.

The wall contains thousands of **watchtowers**, *blockhouses, and beacon towers. The beacon towers were employed to send smoke
25 signals to alert soldiers of enemy attacks. There are additionally gates which permitted passage through the wall. Alongside the wall, there were

barracks for soldiers and **stables** for horses. At times, around one million soldiers protected China's northern frontier from its enemies.

Today, many parts of the wall have fallen into **disrepair**. Nevertheless, large areas still exist, making it a popular tourist attraction, and it remains the world's longest manmade structure. Despite its enormous size, there is no truth to the rumor that the Great Wall of China can be observed from space. When Neil Armstrong landed on the moon in 1969, he mentioned being unable to see it. Words 341

P5 What the wall is like

30 ————————

*blockhouse: a fort with windows that soldiers may fire weapons out of

 Check the main point of the passage.

a. The Great Wall of China is the longest of all defensive walls.

b. There were times when the Great Wall of China failed to protect the country.

c. The Great Wall of China was built for centuries and protected the country.

d. Most of the work on the Great Wall of China was done during the Ming Dynasty.

i When the wall was being made, sometimes peasants worked on it. Other times, soldiers and prisoners built the wall. In some cases, when workers died building the wall, they were simply buried in the wall itself.

Reading Comprehension

1   In paragraph 2, which of the following is NOT mentioned about the Great Wall of China?

   a. The tallest height and average width of its walls

   b. How often the Chinese had to repair it

   c. When the Chinese first began to work on it

   d. The reason that the Chinese decided to build it

2   What does the underlined part in the passage mean?

   a. the design of the wall

   b. the building of the wall

   c. the materials used in the wall

   d. the repairing of the wall

3   According to paragraph 4, which of the following is true about the beacon towers?

   a. They let soldiers know where there was a fire.

   b. They permitted people to pass through the wall.

   c. They were the structures that soldiers got some rest in.

   d. They were used by soldiers to communicate with one another.

4   The word rumor in the passage is closest in meaning to

   a. tale   b. fact   c. fable   d. legend

5   In paragraph 5, which of the following can be inferred about the Great Wall of China?

   a. It looks the same as when it was first built.

   b. It is the most popular tourist attraction in the world.

   c. People thought it was big enough to be seen from space.

   d. Neil Armstrong was the first person to see it from the moon.

6   How long were all the walls that the Chinese built?

The Chinese constructed _____.

7   How did many people who worked on the Great Wall of China die?

_____

Organizing the Passage

Complete the organizer with the phrases in the box.

The Great Wall of China

The Building of the Wall	• The Chinese built the wall because of ❶_____. • Construction began in the seventh century B.C. and continued until ❷_____. • More than ❸_____ of wall were constructed.
The Building Process	• It was built with earth, straw, and tree branches initially and was later made with ❹_____. • Millions of people worked to make the wall, and up to a million died while constructing it.
The Characteristics of the Wall	• It has watchtowers, blockhouses, and beacon towers, and ❺_____ were near it. • It is the world's longest ❻_____ but cannot be seen from the moon.

barracks and stables　　the Ming Dynasty　　warring tribes
21,000 kilometers　　stones and bricks　　manmade structure

Summarizing the Passage

Use the phrases in the box to complete the summary.

seventh century B.C.　　fifteen meters high
is in disrepair　　Qin Shi Huang　　various towers

The Chinese started building the Great Wall of China in the ❶_____ because of
warring tribes. ❷_____, the first emperor of China, worked on it, and so did the
Ming Dynasty. The wall is around six meters wide on average and up to ❸_____.
Earth, straw, tree branches, stones, and bricks were used to build it. Millions of people made
the wall, and up to a million died in the process. The wall has ❹_____ and other
structures. Large parts of it still exist today, but much of it ❺_____.

Unit 12
Gutenberg's Printing Press

Think about the Topic

1 How did people make books hundreds of years ago?

2 In what ways did the printing press change society?

Vocabulary Preview

A **Match the words with their definitions by writing the correct letters in the blanks.**

1 inspire   _____   a. to buy; to get

2 dip   _____   b. to spread; to send

3 effective   _____   c. in motion or progress

4 ambitious   _____   d. having a desire to be successful

5 print run   _____   e. to break into two or more parts

6 acquire   _____   f. to influence or affect in a positive way

7 literacy rate   _____   g. working well; doing one's job properly

8 underway   _____   h. the number of books printed at one time

9 split up   _____   i. the percentage of people able to read and write

10 transmit   _____   j. to put something into a liquid for a short period of time

B **Choose the words that have similar** (*sim.*) **or opposite** (*opp.*) **meanings from the box.**

invent	prevent	numerous

1 develop   _____ *sim.*

2 multiple   _____ *sim.*

3 enable   _____ *opp.*

Background Knowledge

In the Middle Ages and before, all books were made by hand. It could take a year for a person to write a single book. The people writing the books often made mistakes or wrote unclearly, so the quality of books was not always good. Because of the difficulty of making books, there were not many books in existence until the 1400s.

Gutenberg's Printing Press

Q

What is each paragraph mainly about?

P1 _____
before Gutenberg

P2 How Gutenberg's _____ press was different from previous devices

P3 Some of the works Gutenberg (wrote / printed)

P4 Some (causes / effects) of the inventing of the printing press

Writing was invented 5,000 years ago in Sumer. People in cultures such as ancient Egypt, China, and India all developed writing systems, and they later spread around the world. ❶Yet few people ever learned to read and write. ❷They had to be copied by hand, and paper was rare and
5 expensive. ❸Then, history changed thanks to a man named Johannes Gutenberg. ❹

Gutenberg was born in Germany in 1398. Sometime around 1439, he was **inspired** with an idea for a printing press. He began working to develop a machine that would use movable type. Previous devices used
10 wooden blocks. They were then **dipped** in ink and pressed onto paper. But the metal pieces Gutenberg used let him print pages much more quickly. By 1450, he had developed an **effective** printing press.

His machine was capable of printing thousands of pages a day. Prior machines could only print around
15 fifty pages each day. The first work Gutenberg is believed to have printed was a poem. He then printed various religious works. In 1452, he began an **ambitious** project to print multiple copies of the Bible. By 1455, he had finished the first **print run**
20 of what would be called the Gutenberg Bible. There were 180 Bibles, each of which had 1,286 pages and weighed around six kilograms.

▲ A page from the Gutenberg Bible

Printing press technology rapidly spread throughout Europe. Soon, thousands of books were being printed. This dramatically decreased the
25 prices of books, enabling the middle class to **acquire** them. This resulted in more people learning to read, so the **literacy rate** increased.

▲ Johannes Gutenberg

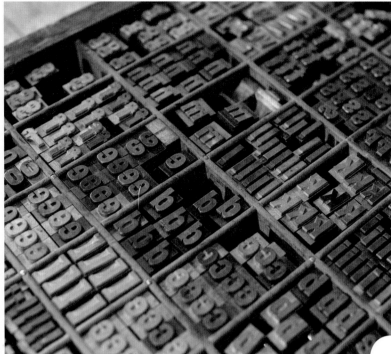
▲ Metal movable type

The Renaissance was already **underway** when Gutenberg made his invention, but the printing press enabled the knowledge learned and relearned in this period to move elsewhere rapidly. It also helped the ideas of the Reformation, which resulted in the **splitting up** of the Roman Catholic Church, to spread. Finally, later periods, such as the Age of Enlightenment and the Industrial Revolution, likely would have happened more slowly—or not at all—had the printing press not let knowledge be **transmitted** so quickly and cheaply. Words 349

30

35

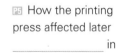
▶ Gutenberg's printing press

P5 How the printing press affected later _____ in history

The movable type Gutenberg invented consisted of metal pieces that looked like letters. He could arrange the pieces so that they created words. Then, he could print as many copies of a page as he wanted.

 Check what the passage is mainly about.

a. How people printed books in the past

b. The reasons that people began to learn to read

c. Gutenberg and the works he published with his printing press

d. How Gutenberg's printing press worked and affected society

Reading Comprehension

1   Where would the following sentence best fit in paragraph 1?

> The primary reason was that there were few books.

a. ❶   b. ❷   c. ❸   d. ❹

2   According to paragraph 2, which of the following is true about Gutenberg's printing press?

a. He worked with a team to invent it.
b. It used wooden blocks to print words.
c. It used movable type to print pages quickly.
d. It took him almost twenty years to develop.

3   In paragraph 3, all of the following questions are answered EXCEPT:

a. When did Gutenberg print the Gutenberg Bible?
b. What was the title of the first work Gutenberg printed?
c. How many copies of the Gutenberg Bible were printed?
d. How many pages could printing presses made prior to Gutenberg's print in one day?

4   The word them in the passage refers to

a. the prices   b. books   c. the middle class   d. more people

5   Which of the following is NOT true about the effects of the printing press?

a. It made the prices of books lower.
b. It helped the literacy rate increase.
c. It made more people trust the Roman Catholic Church.
d. It made the Industrial Revolution happen quickly.

6   How fast could Gutenberg's printing press work?

His machine was capable of printing _____ .

7   How did the printing press affect the Renaissance?

_____

Organizing the Passage

Complete the organizer with the phrases in the box.

	Gutenberg's Printing Press
Before Gutenberg	• Writing was invented 5,000 years ago and existed in ❶_____. • Few people could read and write because books were expensive to make.
The Printing Press	• Gutenberg developed a machine that ❷_____ rather than wooden blocks dipped in ink. • It could print thousands of pages a day. • Gutenberg took three years to print 180 copies of ❸_____.
The Effects of the Printing Press	• ❹_____ decreased, so more people learned to read. • The knowledge learned and relearned during the Renaissance ❺_____. • The ideas of the Reformation spread. • The Age of Enlightenment and ❻_____ happened more quickly.

the prices of books	Egypt, China, and India	the Gutenberg Bible
the Industrial Revolution	spread rapidly	used movable type

Summarizing the Passage

Use the phrases in the box to complete the summary.

Renaissance and Reformation	thousands of pages
read and write	printing press technology	metal pieces

For thousands of years, few people could ❶_____ because books were rare and copied by hand. Then, Johannes Gutenberg invented a printing press that used movable type. It used ❷_____. His printing press could print ❸_____ a day. Gutenberg printed the Gutenberg Bible, and ❹_____ spread rapidly. Thanks to the printing press, more people learned to read, and the ideas of the ❺_____ spread. Other later ages, such as the Age of Enlightenment and the Industrial Revolution, happened more quickly thanks to the printing press.

Chapter 7

Botany

Botany refers to the study of plants, including trees, flowers, bushes, and grasses. Botanists learn about plants and how they live and grow. They also focus on the ecosystems that plants live in and how they interact with their environment, other plants, and animals.

Botany

Unit 13
Plant Diseases

Think about the Topic

1 What are some diseases that plants can get?
2 How do diseases affect some plants?

Vocabulary Preview

A **Match the words with their definitions by writing the correct letters in the blanks.**

1 pathogen _____ a. inactive; in a state of rest

2 fungus (*pl.* fungi) _____ b. a type of animal or plant

3 abnormality _____ c. a basic or necessary food item

4 famine _____ d. causing a great amount of damage

5 staple _____ e. the hard outer covering of a tree

6 dormant _____ f. unable to be harmed by something

7 bark _____ g. a period when there is little food to eat

8 devastating _____ h. something that is unusual or not normal

9 immune _____ i. a virus, bacterium, or anything else that causes a disease

10 strain _____ j. an organism such as a mushroom that grows on plants and has no leaves or flowers

B **Choose the words that have similar** (*sim.*) **or opposite** (*opp.*) **meanings from the box.**

| oppose | hunger | dangerous |

1 harmless _____ *opp.*

2 famine _____ *sim.*

3 resist _____ *sim.*

Background Knowledge

Plants are living organisms, so it is possible for them to get diseases just like humans and animals. Plant diseases may cause a small amount of damage or may kill a plant. In addition, some diseases are contagious and can be passed from plant to plant. This can result in numerous plants dying, which can have a great effect on an ecosystem.

Plant Diseases

Q

What is each paragraph mainly about?

P1 What can cause plants to (catch / get over) diseases

P2 What plant diseases are and how (harmless / severe) they can be

P3 The three main _____ of a plant disease

P4 The types of _____ that plant diseases can cause

Like all living things, plants—both wild and cultivated—can catch diseases. Plant diseases can be caused by **pathogens** such as bacteria, viruses, and **fungi**. To combat them, plants have developed various defenses, and humans have come up with ways to counter them as well.

5   A plant disease is any **abnormality** which disrupts the normal life of a plant. Some can be relatively harmless, but others can result in severe problems. In fact, plant diseases have at times wiped out large areas of crops and caused serious **famines**. This happened in the 1840s when a *blight destroyed the **staple** potato crop in Ireland, which resulted in
10   enormous problems there.

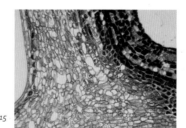

▲ Plant cells infected by pathogens

There are three main stages of a plant disease. The first is when the pathogen enters the plant in some way, such as through an opening in the plant's structure. The second stage happens when the
15   pathogen lies **dormant** inside the plant for a certain period of time as it grows larger or multiplies in number. The third and final stage is infection, which is when symptoms of the disease appear on the plant.

20   At that point, the pathogen begins to weaken the plant, mainly by destroying cells or by blocking the paths of fluids. Depending upon the type of disease, various parts of the plant may be attacked. Some diseases attack roots
25   whereas others cause harm to the stem, leaves, or even the **bark** of trees. The

▲ A chestnut tree

pathogen can also spread to other plants by the third stage. The results of this can be **devastating**. For example, chestnut blight spread rapidly to American chestnut trees and killed millions of them.

Over time, plants have developed ways to resist various diseases, so they have become **immune** to certain problems. In addition, humans often use chemicals to stop and control the spread of plant diseases. And thanks to modern science, disease-resistant **strains** of some plants have been developed. In the future, plant diseases will likely still exist yet will be less harmful to plants. Words 332

30 P5 How plants and humans are developing ways to (resist / cause) various diseases

*blight: a disease that makes plants dry up and die

Scientists are developing genetically modified (GM) plants that can resist diseases. Disease-resistant papayas, squash, and potatoes have all been developed. If scientists can create GM staple crops that can resist diseases, they will increase crop yields in many places.

 Check what the passage is mainly about.

a. The dangers that some diseases pose to plants

b. Plant diseases and why they affect certain plants

c. The best ways to resist and overcome plant diseases

d. The stages of plant diseases and how they harm plants

Reading Comprehension

1 The word cultivated in the passage is closest in meaning to

  a. harvested   b. picked   c. planted   d. used

2 According to paragraphs 2 and 3, which of the following is true about plant diseases?

  a. They have caused periods of starvation for people.

  b. They are harmful and usually cause severe problems.

  c. They first became known to people in Ireland in the 1840s.

  d. They cause problems as soon as pathogens enter the plant.

3 The word it in the passage refers to

  a. the second stage

  b. the pathogen

  c. the plant

  d. a certain period of time

4 In paragraph 4, all of the following questions are answered EXCEPT:

  a. What causes pathogens to spread to other plants?

  b. How do pathogens often cause damage to plants?

  c. Which parts of plants do some diseases attack?

  d. What did chestnut blight do to American chestnut trees?

5 Which of the following can be inferred about plant diseases in paragraph 5?

  a. They will be completely eliminated in the future.

  b. They will become more dangerous as they evolve.

  c. They will become immune to many chemicals people use.

  d. They will not kill as many plants in the future as they do now.

6 What is a plant disease?

  It is _____ .

7 What happens during the infection stage of a plant disease?

  _____

Organizing the Passage

Complete the organizer with the phrases in the box.

Plant Diseases

What They Are	• They are any abnormalities which ❶_____ of a plant. • Some diseases are relatively harmless, but others can cause serious problems, including ❷_____ .
The Three Main Stages of Plant Diseases	• The first is when the pathogen enters the plant. • The second happens when the pathogen ❸_____ in the plant as it grows larger or multiplies in number. • The third happens when the plant is infected and symptoms of the disease appear on it. • The pathogen ❹_____ and attacks various parts of the plant.
Resisting Diseases	• Some plants have ❺_____ to certain problems. • Humans ❻_____ to stop and control the spread of diseases. • They have also developed disease-resistant strains of plants.

become immune severe famines weakens the plant
disrupt the normal life use chemicals lies dormant

Summarizing the Passage

Use the phrases in the box to complete the summary.

three main stages disease-resistant strains
the potato blight catch diseases symptoms appear

Pathogens can cause plants to ❶_____ . These are any abnormalities that disrupt the normal lives of plants. Some diseases are harmless, but others, like ❷_____ in Ireland in the 1840s, can be severe. There are ❸_____ of a plant disease. First, a pathogen enters a plant. Next, the pathogen is dormant as it grows. Finally, ❹_____ on the plant. Plant diseases can affect roots, the stem, leaves, or the bark of plants. Some plants have developed ways to resist diseases while humans are using chemicals and developing ❺_____ of plants.

Unit 14
Hybrid Plants

Think about the Topic

1 Do you know any examples of hybrid plants?
2 How do you think hybrid plants are made?

Vocabulary Preview

A **Match the words with their definitions by writing the correct letters in the blanks.**

1 crossbreed _____ a. a type or kind

2 variety _____ b. to gain; to get

3 countless _____ c. a characteristic

4 robust _____ d. strong and healthy

5 trait _____ e. the science of heredity

6 genetics _____ f. great in number; very many

7 monk _____ g. to do or complete something successfully

8 accomplish _____ h. a member of a religious community of men

9 tissue _____ i. a group of cells with a similar structure and function

10 attain _____ j. to produce a new plant by having two different ones reproduce together

B **Choose the words that have similar (*sim.*) or opposite (*opp.*) meanings from the box.**

| innumerable | artificial | separate |

1 natural _____ *opp.*

2 countless _____ *sim.*

3 attach _____ *opp.*

Background Knowledge

In nature, organisms that are different breeds or species can reproduce to create hybrids. For instance, a horse and a donkey can reproduce to make a mule. A lion and a tiger can produce a liger as their offspring. It is also possible for plants to create hybrids. This can be done through natural means or through the actions of humans.

Hybrid Plants

It is possible to **crossbreed** two **varieties** of the same species of plant to create a new one. Known as a hybrid, this plant often takes on the best qualities of both plants it comes from.

Q

What is each paragraph mainly about?

P2 How humans affected plants through
_____

Natural *hybridization created **countless** plants over a period of millions
5 of years. Then, approximately 10,000 years ago, humans learned to farm. Early farmers noticed that some plants they grew were bigger, stronger, more colorful, and more **robust** than others. They also produced fruits, vegetables, or nuts that were very tasty. Farmers began saving the seeds produced by those plants and planted them the following year.
10 _____, they created better, stronger, and healthier plants.

P3 The work on
_____ done
by Gregor Mendel

The differences in the quality of certain plants were due to their genetic **traits**. It was not until the late nineteenth century that people began understanding
15 **genetics** though. Then, Gregor Mendel, an Austrian **monk**, conducted experiments by crossbreeding pea plants. He kept detailed records of his methods and results. Over time, his work became widely known, providing people
20 with the knowledge needed to create hybrid plants.

▲ Gregor Mendel

P4 The two main ways
_____ can be
accomplished

There are two main ways hybridization can be **accomplished**. One method is to take pollen from a male plant and to transfer it to a female plant of a different variety. The resulting seeds can produce a new plant. It may have characteristics of its parents or be different from them. The
25 second method is grafting. This is done by taking a branch of one plant and attaching it to another plant already growing. The two are bound together,

▲ The grafting of apple trees

and the smaller plant joins its **tissue** with the larger one. In modern times, this method is frequently done with fruit trees.

Many plants grown nowadays are results of hybridization. For example, the corn people eat around the world comes from a small plant originally found in Mexico. It was once shorter than two and a half centimeters long, but through the process of crossbreeding, it **attained** its present form. Thanks to hybrids, there is a diversity of plant life around the world.

30

🔲 The (causes / effects) of hybridization on plants around the world

Words 339

*hybridization: the process of producing a hybrid

 Check what the passage is mainly about.

a. The advantages of hybrid plants

b. Some common hybrid plants

c. Why humans sometimes make hybrid plants

d. Hybrid plants and how they can be made

ⓘ Gregor Mendel experimented with peas, particularly with regard to the colors of the flowers they produced. Thanks to his work, dominant and recessive characteristics were discovered. His work was rejected by others while he was alive, but it is highly respected today.

Reading Comprehension

1 The word They in the passage refers to

    a. Humans   b. Early farmers   c. Some plants   d. Others

2 What is the best choice for the blank?

    a. In addition

    b. In doing so

    c. In spite of this

    d. In other words

3 Which of the following is NOT true according to paragraph 3?

    a. Mendel crossbred pea plants for his experiments.

    b. Mendel's work on genetics became famous immediately.

    c. People did not understand genetics in the eighteenth century.

    d. Genetic traits are responsible for different qualities of plants.

4 According to paragraph 4, which of the following is true about grafting?

    a. It is done by connecting a branch of one plant to another.

    b. It was a popular way of producing fruit trees in the past.

    c. It requires pollen to be taken from one plant and transferred to another.

    d. It can be done by binding two different branches of a tree to each other.

5 In paragraph 5, which of the following is mentioned about hybridization?

    a. How people learned to do it

    b. Where it first occurred

    c. How long it usually takes

    d. What one result of it is

6 What happened around 10,000 years ago?

Approximately 10,000 years ago, _____ .

7 What was a result of the work Gregor Mendel did?

_____

Organizing the Passage

Complete the organizer with the phrases in the box.

	Hybrid Plants
Hybridization	• It ❶_____ over a period of millions of years. • When humans learned to farm 10,000 years ago, farmers began saving seeds from the best plants. • They planted the seeds and created better, ❷_____ plants.
Gregor Mendel	• He did ❸_____ by crossbreeding pea plants. • He provided people with the knowledge needed to ❹_____.
Two Ways to Create Hybrids	• The first is to take pollen from a male plant and to transfer it to ❺_____ of a different variety. • The seeds created from that then make a new plant. • Grafting is done by taking a branch of one plant and ❻_____ to another plant that is growing. • The smaller plant joins its tissue with the larger one.

happened naturally	a female plant	create hybrid plants
stronger, and healthier	work on genetics	attaching it

Summarizing the Passage

Use the phrases in the box to complete the summary.

plant diversity	can be crossbred	
graft a branch	how to farm	taking pollen

   Two varieties of the same species of plant ❶_____ to create a hybrid plant. This can be done naturally or by people. Humans have been doing this ever since they learned ❷_____. The genetics were not understood until Gregor Mendel crossbred pea plants. He showed people how to create hybrids. Some are created by ❸_____ from one species and transferring it to a female plant of a different variety. It is also possible to ❹_____ of one plant onto another plant. There is a lot of ❺_____ nowadays thanks to hybridization.

Chapter **8**

Physics

Physics refers to the study of matter and energy and how they interact with each other. Physicists study a number of different things, including electricity, motion, light, gravity, and radiation. They often observe the natural world and try to understand the forces that are at work in it.

Unit 15

Water and Wind Currents

Think about the Topic

1 What is the wind, and how does is blow?

2 Why does water move?

Vocabulary Preview

A **Match the words with their definitions by writing the correct letters in the blanks.**

1 interaction _____ a. a long, thin strip

2 ripple _____ b. straight up from a surface

3 parallel _____ c. moving from place to place

4 horizontally _____ d. a small wave in a body of water

5 vertically _____ e. in a way that is flat or level to the ground

6 density _____ f. the effect that one thing has on another

7 salinity _____ g. the mass of something per unit of volume

8 rotation _____ h. the movement of a body as it turns around

9 circulating _____ i. the amount of salt in a liquid such as water

10 band _____ j. moving in the same direction, always being the same distance at every point, and never meeting

B **Choose the words that have similar** (*sim.*) **or opposite** (*opp.*) **meanings from the box.**

bend   fall   run into

1 rise _____ *opp.*

2 curve _____ *sim.*

3 encounter _____ *sim.*

Background Knowledge

Air and water on the Earth can remain steady, but they can also be in motion. When the wind blows constantly in a certain direction and water moves constantly in a certain direction, wind currents and water currents, respectively, are formed. Both types of currents can have major effects on the Earth.

Water and Wind Currents

Q

What is each paragraph mainly about?

P1 (What / Where) currents are

P2 Where water currents happen and how they can _____

P3 What affects the formation of water currents and how they can _____

P4 What (influences / warms) wind currents and how they are created

Currents are moving masses of air and water caused due to the **interactions** of various forces. They combine with one another and move air and water in great amounts or volumes around the world.

Most water currents happen in the world's oceans, but there are also
5 currents in seas, rivers, and streams. The most common ones are located near the surface and are caused by blowing winds. As the wind moves across the water's surface, it causes **ripples**, which then form waves. When the waves reach the shore at an angle, they form strong currents that move **parallel** to the land.

10 Other ocean currents take place farther beneath the surface of the ocean when water moves either **horizontally** or **vertically**. For instance, cold water sinks while
15 warm water rises. The **density** and **salinity** of water also affect how ocean currents form. Finally, the Earth's **rotation** plays a role in where currents form and how they move.
20 The rotation causes most currents

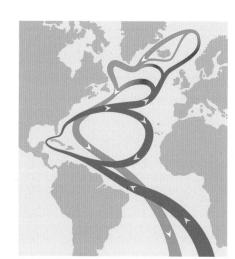

▲ The Gulf Stream Current

to curve rather than to move in a straight line. For instance, the Gulf Stream Current in the Atlantic Ocean moves up the coast of North America. It then crosses the Atlantic and goes to Europe.

As for wind currents, they are influenced by temperature, density, air
25 pressure, and the Earth's rotation. The sun warms the Earth's surface, causing heat to rise. As heat moves upward, it forms a low atmospheric

pressure area. In cooler areas, high pressure regions form. Air then moves from high pressure areas to low pressure ones, thereby creating winds.

The Earth's rotation creates large areas of **circulating** winds in the upper atmosphere. These circulating air currents create global weather patterns. Another type of air current is the jet stream. When a large mass of heated air encounters very cold air high in the atmosphere, a powerful stream of moving air is created. The jet stream moves from west to east in a narrow **band** at speeds of more than 300 kilometers per hour. This increases flight times for planes traveling west, but thanks to strong *tailwinds, planes flying eastward can reach their destinations quickly. Words 350

30

35

What the _____ is and how it moves

*tailwind: a wind that blows behind a moving object and pushes it forward

 Check the main point of the passage.

a. There are many wind currents but only a few water currents.

b. Currents of wind and water form due to various factors.

c. The wind moves horizontally while water moves vertically.

d. Wind currents are more powerful than water currents.

i Sometimes water piles up on beaches instead of flowing away from waves that hit shore. In those cases, rip currents can form when the water suddenly rushes back out to sea. These are extremely powerful and dangerous and kill around 100 people each year.

Reading Comprehension

1 The word it in the passage refers to

    a. the wind

    c. the shore

    b. the water's surface

    d. an angle

2 According to paragraph 2, which of the following is true about water currents?

    a. Most of them are found deep beneath the surface.

    b. They can make ripples form on the water's surface.

    c. They can form in bodies of water other than oceans.

    d. They make the wind blow from the ocean to the land.

3 Why does the author mention the Gulf Stream Current?

    a. To show the route it takes across the ocean

    b. To compare it with another famous current

    c. To state that it affects the Earth's rotation

    d. To point out that the water in it moves vertically

4 In paragraph 4, which of the following is NOT mentioned about wind currents?

    a. What they can be affected by

    b. How heat helps create them

    c. The role of the sun in forming them

    d. The speeds that they may move

5 According to paragraph 5, which of the following is true about the jet stream?

    a. It affects global weather patterns.

    b. The Earth's rotation mainly causes it to form.

    c. It sometimes moves down near the ground.

    d. It makes flights longer or shorter depending on the direction.

6 What are currents?

Currents are _____.

7 When do ocean currents take place farther beneath the surface of ocean?

_____

Organizing the Passage

Select the appropriate statements from the answer choices and match them to the type of current to which they relate. Two of the answer choices will NOT be used.

Water Current	Wind Current
•	•
•	•
•	

1 Can move horizontally or vertically

2 May move parallel to land in some instances

3 May form for a short time and then suddenly disappear

4 Has been known to move completely around the world

5 Has its movement partially affected by the rotation of the Earth

6 Is able to move faster than 300 kilometers per hour in some cases

7 Is affected by temperature, density, air pressure, and the Earth's rotation

Summarizing the Passage

Use the phrases in the box to complete the summary.

the Earth's rotation	can move faster
beneath the surface	high pressure areas	moving masses

Currents are ❶_____ of air or water. Most water currents are in oceans and are most commonly near the surface. Other water currents may form deep ❷_____ of the ocean and may move horizontally or vertically. ❸_____ makes currents like the Gulf Stream Current curve as they move. Wind currents are affected by temperature, density, air pressure, and the Earth's rotation. They form when air moves from ❹_____ to ones with low pressure. The jet stream is an air current high in the atmosphere that ❺_____ than 300 kilometers per hour.

Unit 16
Gravity in the Solar System

Think about the Topic

1 What is gravity?

2 How does gravity affect objects on other planets?

Vocabulary Preview

A Match the words with their definitions by writing the correct letters in the blanks.

1 invisible _____ a. together with

2 mass _____ b. to keep or remain

3 exert _____ c. unable to be seen

4 noticeable _____ d. to put forth or use

5 orbit (n.) _____ e. able to be seen

6 asteroid _____ f. different in degree, size, etc.

7 in conjunction with _____ g. the quantity of matter as determined by its weight

8 tide _____ h. the periodic rising and falling of the water in the sea

9 maintain _____ i. one of the many small objects that move around the sun

10 unequal _____ j. a curved path a planet or a moon follows as it moves around the sun or another planet

B Choose the words that have similar (*sim.*) **or opposite** (*opp.*) **meanings from the box.**

strengthen	coast	obvious

1 noticeable _____ *sim.*

2 weaken _____ *opp.*

3 shoreline _____ *sim.*

Background Knowledge

The solar system includes the sun and everything that is affected by its gravity. Among these are the eight planets—Mercury, Venus, Earth, Mars, Jupiter, Saturn, Uranus, and Neptune—and their moons. There are also several dwarf planets like Pluto as well as countless asteroids, meteors, and comets.

Gravity in the Solar System

Q

What is each paragraph mainly about?

P1 What _____ is

P2 What (effects / uses) gravity has on objects in the solar system

P3 The effects gravity has on the moon's (density / orbit) and the Earth's tides

P4 How gravity affects the planets and why its _____ is different

Gravity is an **invisible** force of attraction that pulls all objects in the universe toward one another. The bigger an object's **mass**, the more gravity it has. Gravity is at its strongest when two objects are close and weakens as they move _____.

5   While small objects have gravity, the pull they **exert** on other objects is so tiny that it cannot be measured. Gravity's effects are **noticeable**, though, in large objects such as stars, planets, and moons. In fact, it plays a key role in the structure of the solar system because the sun's gravity keeps the planets in **orbit**. Its gravity also influences other objects, including **asteroids**
10 and comets.

Earth's gravity keeps the moon in constant orbit around it. The moon also has gravity, yet its gravity is equal to roughly one-sixth of Earth's. The
15 moon's gravity—**in conjunction with** that of the sun—is still strong enough to create **tides** on the Earth's bodies of water. Their gravity pulls at the oceans, seas, and some lakes, causing water to
20 rise and fall along shorelines.

Most other planets in the solar system have moons, all of which are **maintained** in orbit by their planets' gravitational forces. Every planet has gravity, but it differs in strength because the force of gravity depends upon an object's mass and density. On the Earth, gravity equals 1g, which is the
25 measurement of the planet's gravity.

Scientists use this standard to measure gravity on other planets. For example, Mercury is smaller than Earth but nearly as dense, so its gravitational force is just over one-third of Earth's at 0.38g. Venus is almost the same size and density as Earth, so its gravity is 0.9g. This means a man weighing 100 kilograms would feel like he weighs 90 kilograms on Venus. Jupiter is huge, so its gravity is approximately 2.5 times that of Earth's. That same man would feel like he weighs 250 kilograms on Jupiter.

30

Every object in the solar system possesses **unequal** forces of gravity. However, gravity works the same way, so it is easy to measure and to understand its effects. Words 350

P5 How strong or weak gravity is on other

_____

Even though Saturn, Uranus, and Neptune are much bigger than Earth, they are less dense because they are mostly made of gas. So their gravity is similar to Earth's. The sun, on the other hand, is massive, so its gravity is 30 times greater than Earth's.

 Check the main point of the passage.

a. The force of gravity causes the tides to happen on the Earth.

b. Not all of the planets have gravity that is as strong as the Earth's.

c. Gravity is a powerful force that affects every object in the solar system.

d. The planets and moons maintain their orbits because of gravity.

Reading Comprehension

1 What is the best choice for the blank?

   a. faster and faster

   b. farther away

   c. next to each other

   d. around the sun

2 Which of the following is true according to paragraphs 1 and 2?

   a. Every object in the universe has strong gravity.

   b. The distance between objects does not affect gravity.

   c. The sun's gravity makes the planets in the solar system go around it.

   d. The sun is responsible for the formation of comets and asteroids.

3 Why does the author mention tides?

   a. To claim that they only exist on the Earth

   b. To show one effect of the moon's gravity

   c. To show how long they last each day

   d. To explain how strong they are in some places

4 The word measurement in the passage is closest in meaning to

   a. altitude   b. system   c. size   d. appearance

5 In paragraph 5, all of the following questions are answered EXCEPT:

   a. How powerful is the force of gravity on Mercury?

   b. Why does Jupiter have such a powerful force of gravity?

   c. Would a person from Earth feel like he weighs more on the moon or Mars?

   d. Which planet in the solar system has a size and a density similar to Earth's?

6 How much would a man weighing 100 kilograms feel like he weighs on Venus?

   A man weighing 100 kilograms would feel like _____.

7 Why does the gravity of each planet differ in strength?

_____

Organizing the Passage

Complete the organizer with the phrases in the box.

Gravity in the Solar System	
What Gravity Is	• It is an invisible force of attraction that pulls all objects in the universe ❶ _____ . • It is stronger when ❷ _____ and weakens as they move farther away. • Small objects have weak gravity, but large ones like ❸ _____ have strong gravity.
Earth and the Moon	• It keeps the moon in orbit around the Earth. • The moon's gravity ❹ _____ on the Earth's bodies of water.
The Planets in the Solar System	• Their ❺ _____ by their mass and density. • Mercury has a gravitational force a bit ❻ _____ of Earth's. • Venus's gravity is almost the same as Earth's, but Jupiter's is 2.5 times that of Earth's.

two objects are close	gravity is determined	toward one another
stars, planets, and moons	more than one-third	affects the tides

Summarizing the Passage

Use the phrases in the box to complete the summary.

its mass and density	the gravitational forces	
Mercury and Venus	force of attraction	keeps the moon

Gravity is the ❶ _____ that makes objects pull one another toward them. Its effects are noticeable for large objects. Earth's gravity ❷ _____ in orbit around it while the moon's gravity affects the tides on the Earth. Moons are maintained in orbit by ❸ _____ of the planets that they go around. The gravity of each planet differs in strength and is determined by ❹ _____ . ❺ _____ have gravity weaker than Earth's, but Jupiter's gravity is 2.5 times greater than Earth's.

TOEFL
Practice Test

Suburbs and Exurbs

Washington, D.C. in the United States is a major metropolitan center with around 600,000 people. Near it are the cities Arlington, Alexandria, and Springfield. They are all suburbs of Washington. Moving farther outward, there are Fredericksburg City, Stafford County, and Spotsylvania County. These places—and others near them—are exurbs of Washington.

The first suburbs formed around the 1850s. Cities such as London, England, became enormous during the 1800s. Because these urban centers were so large, people began moving to areas outside them. These places were called suburbs. Over time, many suburbs themselves grew to be large in size. So roughly one hundred years later in the 1950s, people started moving from the suburbs to the exurbs. These are more rural areas found outside suburbs.

Today, there is a distinct divide between suburbs and exurbs. They differ in their locations, facilities, and services and in the quality of life their residents have. Regarding locations, suburbs are closer to urban centers and, in fact, normally border them. Exurbs, on the other hand, are often in rural areas or by beaches. Suburbs tend to have larger populations than exurbs on account of their locations.

Suburbs have most of the facilities found in urban areas. They have well-developed road systems as well as public transportation such as buses, subways, and commuter rails. ■ There are shopping centers, restaurants, entertainment areas, and commercial and business facilities in them. ■ Exurbs may have large areas dedicated to farming. ■ They have few businesses and commercial centers, and their residents rely on private transportation to get around. ■

People are attracted to suburbs since they contain many of the advantages of cities yet are not as crowded. There are disadvantages, too, including high crime rates and pollution. Exurbs are for people who value their independence and enjoy quiet places. Their crime rates are also much lower.

There are people who prefer suburbs and those who like living in exurbs better. Each has its benefits and drawbacks. Most people choose to live in them based upon the type of life and the quality of life they wish to lead.

1   **In paragraph 1, all of the following questions are answered EXCEPT:**

   Ⓐ What is the population of Washington, D.C.?
   Ⓑ Which cities near Washington, D.C. are considered suburbs?
   Ⓒ What type of place is Stafford County considered to be?
   Ⓓ How many suburbs and exurbs does Washington, D.C. have?

2 **In paragraph 2, the author implies that suburbs**

 Ⓐ took more than a hundred years to grow large

 Ⓑ are losing popularity to big cities and exurbs

 Ⓒ had more people in the 1900s than they did in the 1800s

 Ⓓ cost less money to live in than urban centers

3 **The word "them" in the passage refers to**

 Ⓐ their residents

 Ⓑ locations

 Ⓒ suburbs

 Ⓓ urban centers

4 **Where would the following sentence best fit in paragraph 4?**

As a result, people can travel from them to nearby cities both quickly and easily.

5 **According to paragraph 5, which of the following is true about exurbs?**

 Ⓐ Some places tend to be crowded.

 Ⓑ They usually have high levels of pollution.

 Ⓒ Their residents may live close to one another.

 Ⓓ Crime is not much of a problem in them.

6 **Select the appropriate statements from the answer choices and match them to the location to which they relate. Two of the answer choices will NOT be used.**

STATEMENTS	LOCATION
❶ Can be found both in rural locations and near the beach	**Suburb** (Select 2)
❷ Is the fastest-growing type of place in many countries	• •
❸ Requires its residents to use their own vehicles to move around	
❹ Has shopping centers, businesses, and public transportation like cities	**Exurb** (Select 3)
❺ Tends to be overcrowded with people living close to one another	• • •
❻ May have large amounts of pollution as well as crime	
❼ Has many places that are used for agriculture	

The Montessori Method

For centuries, much teaching was done through rote learning. This required the memorizing of facts through repetition. One educator, Maria Montessori, came up with a new method of learning. It focused on experiential learning and the natural development of children. It would be called the Montessori Method after her.

Montessori herself was a teacher. She created her teaching method while working at a school for disabled children. Her method had several notable features. One was that children could learn at their own pace. This gave them a great amount of independence when it came to learning. In addition, she let children of various ages share the same classroom. Finally, she focused on what was called practical play. It let students learn by doing various activities. The types of activities students did were based upon three separate age groups.

The first group is from birth to the age of three. In this group, learners are encouraged by teachers to focus on their senses and their immediate environment. Teachers help learners develop their motor skills, coordination, and language skills. They use repetition, the manipulation of objects, and the exploration of the world around them to do this. Students also do hands-on activities to learn.

The second group is learners from ages three to six. These learners also focus on using their senses and working with objects in their daily lives. Teachers encourage learners to be independent and creative. There is a focus on reading and mathematics. And students learn to play with others. In fact, collaborative activities, such as role-playing, help learners get along with others and develop various skills.

The third group comprises learners ages six to twelve. Teachers determine learners' interests and guide and support them as they pursue knowledge in those fields. Learners also develop their imaginations and self-confidence and learn abstract concepts. Finally, learners are taught about their roles in their local communities, their cultures, and the entire world.

The Montessori method became a popular way for many children to learn. Today, schools around the world use it to teach students and to develop their skills.

1   **The word "memorizing" in the passage is closest in meaning to**

Ⓐ appreciating   Ⓑ considering   Ⓒ reciting   Ⓓ remembering

2 **In paragraphs 1 and 2, which of the following is NOT true about the Montessori Method?**

Ⓐ It acquired its name due to the person who created it.

Ⓑ It divides learners into four separate age groups.

Ⓒ It promotes students doing activities in order to learn.

Ⓓ It allows students to work as fast or as slow as they want.

3 **In paragraph 3, why does the author mention "hands-on activities"?**

Ⓐ To describe some specific skills that young learners do

Ⓑ To name something that young children do to learn

Ⓒ To contrast them with the language skills that children learn

Ⓓ To point out that only very young children do them

4 **According to paragraph 4, teachers have learners work together because**

Ⓐ they can gain knowledge much faster that way

Ⓑ group activities are considered to be very important

Ⓒ doing that allows learners to become independent

Ⓓ it shows them how to be friends with other learners

5 **Which of the sentences below best expresses the essential information in the highlighted sentence in the passage?** *Incorrect* **answer choices change the meaning in important ways or leave out essential information.**

Teachers determine learners' interests and guide and support them as they pursue knowledge in those fields.

Ⓐ Learners are able to pursue knowledge in a wide variety of fields.

Ⓑ There are several teachers who can help learners study different subjects.

Ⓒ Students must have support from teachers if they want to be able to learn well.

Ⓓ Teachers help students learn after figuring out what they are interested in.

6 **An introductory sentence for a brief summary of the passage is provided below. Complete the summary by selecting the THREE answer choices that express the most important ideas of the passage.**

The Montessori Method helps young children learn in various ways.

❶ As students get older, they learn abstract ideas as well as their place in the world.

❷ Students often enjoy school more if they study by using the Montessori Method.

❸ Maria Montessori came up with the Montessori Method while teaching at a school.

❹ Students focus on their senses and the environment as well as hands-on learning.

❺ Children of various ages study together and are able to learn at their own pace.

Pax Romana

For centuries, Rome existed as a *republic. Then, during the first century B.C., a civil war occurred there. After it concluded, Rome was no longer a republic but an empire. Rome then entered a phase in its history called the Pax Romana, Latin for "Roman Peace."

Beginning in 60 B.C., three men—Julius Caesar, Pompey, and Crassus—dominated Rome and ruled together in what was called the First Triumvirate. Crassus was defeated in battle and killed in 53 B.C., so only two men remained. There was eventually a civil war between Caesar and Pompey. Caesar emerged victorious and became the dictator of Rome in 45 B.C. However, Caesar was assassinated in the Roman Senate on March 15, 44 B.C.

This resulted in another group of three men—Octavian, Lepidus, and Marc Antony—becoming powerful and forming the Second Triumvirate. However, they constantly battled one another, and when the fighting concluded, only Octavian remained. In 27 B.C., he was named emperor of Rome and changed his name to Augustus. This marked the beginning of the Roman Empire as well as the Pax Romana.

This was not entirely a peaceful time since Rome was almost constantly at war with outside forces and periodically expanded its borders. However, the people of the empire were at peace with one another as there were no civil wars during this time. During the Pax Romana, the Romans built numerous great structures, including the Colosseum in Rome and Hadrian's Wall in Britain. A network of roads was constructed that connected every part of the empire with Rome. There was also a Silver Age of Roman literature as great works were written then. Men like Tacitus and Suetonius wrote histories, Seneca penned rhetoric, and Juvenal and Petronius created satires, all of which are still read in modern times.

The Pax Romana lasted for approximately 200 years until it ended in 180 A.D. with the death of Emperor Marcus Aurelius. The empire itself would continue until 476, but it would never reach the heights it did during the Pax Romana.

*republic: a state where citizens vote for representatives who then rule according to the will of the people

1   **The word "phase" in the passage is closest in meaning to**

   Ⓐ plot   Ⓑ stage   Ⓒ climax   Ⓓ group

2 **According to paragraph 2, which of the following is true about the First Triumvirate?**

Ⓐ It lasted from the years 60 B.C. to 44 B.C.

Ⓑ A dictator of Rome was established due to it.

Ⓒ Rome lost some territory while it lasted.

Ⓓ The three members made Rome very powerful.

3 **Which of the following can be inferred from paragraph 3 about Octavian?**

Ⓐ He was closely related to Julius Caesar.

Ⓑ He was able to defeat both Lepidus and Marc Antony.

Ⓒ He was responsible for forming the Second Triumvirate.

Ⓓ He went by the name Augustus before he became emperor.

4 **In paragraph 4, the author's description of the Pax Romana mentions all of the following EXCEPT:**

Ⓐ Several writers who became famous for their work

Ⓑ The type of peace that existed during that time

Ⓒ The names of some emperors who ruled then

Ⓓ Some of the structures that were made during it

5 **In paragraph 4, the author uses "Juvenal and Petronius" as examples of**

Ⓐ authors who were skilled in several forms of writing

Ⓑ the Roman writers most remembered in modern times

Ⓒ two people who were the first to write in the satire genre

Ⓓ great writers of the Silver Age of Roman literature

6 **An introductory sentence for a brief summary of the passage is provided below. Complete the summary by selecting the THREE answer choices that express the most important ideas of the passage.**

> The Pax Romana was a great period in Roman history and happened after a time of civil war.

❶ Octavian, Lepidus, and Marc Antony combined to form the Second Triumvirate.

❷ There was a great deal of fighting during the First Triumvirate and the Second Triumvirate.

❸ The Romans made impressive structures and works of literature during the Pax Romana.

❹ Julius Caesar became the dictator of Rome but was assassinated in the Roman Senate.

❺ The Pax Romana lasted for nearly 200 years from the time of Octavian to Marcus Aurelius.

Land Reclamation

Humans tend to live near water. As settlements grow, so too does the need for land. So people have learned to reclaim land from lakes, rivers, and oceans. Likewise, land may suffer damage due to natural means or human actions. As a result, people frequently reclaim land to help preserve or restore natural environments.

Land reclamation near waterways can turn places covered by water into inhabitable land. The people of Holland, a country in Europe, have engaged in land reclamation since at least the 1300s. Today, only fifty percent of the country's total area is one meter or higher above sea level. The Dutch people use an intricate system of dikes to remove sea water to reclaim land. Today, around seventeen percent of the land in Holland has been reclaimed from oceans and lakes.

Singapore, a tiny city-state in Southeast Asia, has engaged in land reclamation since the 1960s. It increased its size by nine percent by the 1990s and is reclaiming more land today. Land there is mostly reclaimed by pouring large amounts of dirt and sand onto swamps and ocean water.

The other type of land reclamation can heal land damaged in some way. Erosion, desertification, and mining are three common causes. In the case of mining, land may be contaminated by chemicals. As a result, neither plants nor animals can live on it. By reclaiming the land, often by trucking in large amounts of soil from elsewhere, it can be made fertile again.

Beaches in places such as Cape Cod in Massachusetts, USA, are constantly being eroded by the ocean. ■ Beach nourishment can prevent more erosion and even restore some of the land that has been lost. ■ As for desertification, the Sahara Desert in Africa has been expanding in recent years. ■ Efforts to reclaim the land lost to the desert are preventing the desert from getting too large. ■

By engaging in land reclamation, people can change the face of the Earth. This can provide more land to live on. It can also restore the land to how it previously looked.

1 **According to paragraph 1, people often reclaim land to**

Ⓐ expand the territory of some countries

Ⓑ return the environment to a previous condition

Ⓒ provide more places for wild animals to live on

Ⓓ remove pollution that was created by others

2 **The word "inhabitable" in the passage is closest in meaning to**

Ⓐ clean   Ⓑ dry   Ⓒ beautiful   Ⓓ usable

3 **In paragraph 3, the author's description of Singapore mentions all of the following EXCEPT:**

Ⓐ How land there is being reclaimed

Ⓑ When it started to reclaim land

Ⓒ The way people there are using reclaimed land

Ⓓ The amount of land that has been reclaimed

4 **In paragraph 4, the author uses "Erosion, desertification, and mining" as examples of**

Ⓐ problems that may require people to reclaim land

Ⓑ human activities that are causing harm to the environment

Ⓒ reasons that the land may get contaminated with chemicals

Ⓓ activities that may make plants and animals in areas die

5 **Where would the following sentence best fit in paragraph 5?**

This is the process of adding sand to beaches in order to make them wider.

6 **An introductory sentence for a brief summary of the passage is provided below. Complete the summary by selecting the THREE answer choices that express the most important ideas of the passage.**

It is possible to reclaim land from the water and to fix environmental damage.

❶ Mining can often result in a great amount of contamination to the land.

❷ Erosion and desertification can often be reversed when people reclaim land.

❸ Singapore is one place that has reclaimed land from the ocean to expand its territory.

❹ A large amount of land in Holland has been reclaimed by using a system of dikes.

❺ Many people reside near waterways, so they are often in need of more places to live.

MEMO

MEMO

MEMO

Building Background Knowledge for Academic Subjects

Fundamental Reading

Workbook

PLUS **3**

DARAKWON

Building Background Knowledge for Academic Subjects

Fundamental Reading

Michael A. Putlack
Stephen Poirier
Tony Covello

Workbook

PLUS 3

DARAKWON

Unit 1 How Movies Affect Culture

Vocabulary

A **Read the sentences and choose the best words for the blanks.**

1 Because it was a **profitable** film, it _____ a lot of money.

   a. spent   b. made   c. lost   d. cost

2 The actor features **prominently** in the film, so he is _____ most scenes.

   a. noticeable in   b. missing from   c. speaking in   d. aware of

3 The **impact** of that movie was that it had a great _____ on how people dressed.

   a. size   b. time   c. awareness   d. effect

B **Choose the words from the box to complete the sentences.**

disco music	exploded	arguably	terrorizes	revenues

1 Action movies _____ in popularity in the 1980s.

2 The monster in the movie _____ an entire city.

3 Some movies have _____ on their soundtracks.

4 In the 1970s, *Star Wars* was _____ the most influential movie.

5 Some movies have _____ of more than one billion dollars nowadays.

Translation

C **Read the sentences and translate them into your language.**

1 The purchases shoppers make can additionally be affected by movies.

   → _____

2 Some people have been known to imitate the extreme violence they have seen on the big screen.

   → _____

3 These are essentially commercial advertisements since the hope is that when viewers see these products in movies, they will buy them.

   → _____

Paraphrasing

D **Paraphrase the sentences from the passage with the words and phrases in the box.**

possibly	make lots of money	a negative effect	affect
as for	somewhat helped	people visiting beaches	in film

1 In addition to being highly profitable, movies can also influence the culture.

→ Movies cannot only _____ but can also _____ the culture.

2 It negatively impacted some businesses that relied on tourists going to the beach.

→ It had _____ on businesses that made money from _____.

3 Regarding music, the 1977 movie *Saturday Night Fever* was partly responsible for increasing the popularity of disco music.

→ _____ music, the 1977 movie *Saturday Night Fever* _____ make disco music more popular.

4 Arguably the most successful example of product placement happened in the movie *E.T. the Extra-Terrestrial*.

→ _____ the most successful product placement _____ was in *E.T. the Extra-Terrestrial*.

Listening

E **Listen to the summary and fill in the blanks.**

Movies are a popular ❶ _____ of entertainment that can ❷ _____ culture. Some movies, such as *Annie Hall* and *Back to the Future*, affected ❸ _____ styles. Others, like *Saturday Night Fever*, ❹ _____ the ❺ _____ of disco music. Shoppers can also be influenced by product ❻ _____ in movies. The candy Reese's Pieces became very popular when it ❼ _____ in *E.T. the Extra-Terrestrial*. Movies can also ❽ _____ affect culture. *Jaws* made people afraid of the water, so people avoided going to the beach. Other movies make smoking look cool and contain violent ❾ _____ that some people ❿ _____.

Unit 2 Painting Techniques of the Renaissance

Vocabulary

A   **Read the sentences and choose the best words for the blanks.**

1 He **dramatically** improved his skills by practicing _____.
   a. very much   b. sometimes   c. alone   d. rarely

2 The Middle Ages was a **spiritual** time, so many people were _____.
   a. adventurous   b. violent   c. realistic   d. religious

3 Her use of **shadow** impressed everyone by how the _____ affected the picture.
   a. content   b. darkness   c. images   d. colors

B   **Choose the words from the box to complete the sentences.**

frescoes	precision	scale	reintroduced	depict

1 All of the figures in the picture are drawn to _____.

2 The artist makes his realistic paintings with _____.

3 She plans to _____ a scene from nature in her next painting.

4 The Renaissance _____ learning that had been lost to the West.

5 Michelangelo created beautiful _____ in the Sistine Chapel in the Vatican.

Translation

C   **Read the sentences and translate them into your language.**

1 They emphasized the uses of shadows and light to bring life to their paintings.

   → _____

2 The Renaissance was a period of time in Europe which lasted from approximately 1400 to 1600.

   → _____

3 The Renaissance was an age of humanism, so artwork did not always focus on religious themes.

   → _____

Paraphrasing

D **Paraphrase the sentences from the passage with the phrases in the box.**

how artists painted	have height, width	once again
lacked depth	lost knowledge	great changes

1 Most of the artwork done in the Middle Ages was flat and two dimensional.

→ The artwork of the Middle Ages was usually flat and _____.

2 Artists used a painting method called perspective to give their works a three-dimensional appearance.

→ Artists used perspective to make their paintings _____, and depth.

3 Because of the knowledge that was reintroduced, the way many artists painted changed dramatically.

→ Thanks to the knowledge that was reintroduced, _____ underwent

_____.

4 One feature of that period was that people began to relearn knowledge from ancient Greece and Rome that had been lost over time.

→ A characteristic of that time was that people began to _____ learn _____ from ancient Greece and Rome.

Listening

E **Listen to the summary and fill in the blanks.**

The Renaissance was a period of ❶ _____ that lasted from around 1400 to 1600. The Middle Ages happened before the Renaissance. It was a ❷ _____ age, and artists mostly created ❸ _____ art that was flat and two ❹ _____. The Renaissance used knowledge ❺ _____ from ancient Greece and Rome. It was an age of humanism, so regular people and characters from ❻ _____ were ❼ _____. Artists used different ❽ _____, too. ❾ _____ made their works look three dimensional. They also used shadows and light as well as mathematical ❿ _____.

Unit 3 **Bipolar Disorder**

Vocabulary

A **Read the sentences and choose the best words for the blanks.**

1 The troubled man committed **suicide** and _____ himself last night.

   a. yelled at   b. rewarded   c. killed   d. punished

2 The doctor **prescribed** some _____ for the patient to make her get better.

   a. exercise   b. surgery   c. advice   d. medicine

3 The **psychiatrist** recommended that Mr. Jackson see another _____ for his problem.

   a. patient   b. doctor   c. scientist   d. researcher

B **Choose the words from the box to complete the sentences.**

mood swings	imbalance	resort to	breakthrough	cure

1 The doctor may have to _____ surgery to help the man.

2 The patient's problem was caused by a(n) _____ in her body.

3 The doctor found a(n) _____ for the patient's problem and healed him.

4 The psychologist made a(n) _____ that should help thousands of people.

5 The patient suffers from _____ and can suddenly be happy or depressed.

Translation

C **Read the sentences and translate them into your language.**

1 They are also recommended to plan activities they enjoy to get a sense of fulfillment.

   → _____

2 Until a breakthrough is made, millions of people will suffer from this issue every year.

   → _____

3 Individuals with bipolar disorder experience mood swings that make them feel anywhere from being very happy to being very sad.

   → _____

Paraphrasing

D   **Paraphrase the sentences from the passage with the words and phrases in the box.**

annually	lower	speaking fast	stress levels
approximately	healed them	unable to focus	cease taking it

1   Doctors encourage patients to decrease the amount of stress in their lives.

→ Doctors advise patients to _____ their _____.

2   In the United States alone, it is estimated that roughly six million people suffer from it each year.

→ Just in the United States, _____ six million people suffer from it _____.

3   Many sufferers believe the medicine has made them better, so they stop taking it after a while.

→ Many patients think the medicine _____, so they _____.

4   Some of the most common symptoms of it are thinking and talking quickly, changing one's mind almost instantly, and an inability to concentrate.

→ Some common symptoms are thinking and _____, instantly changing one's mind, and being _____.

Listening

E   **Listen to the summary and fill in the blanks.**

There are many ❶ _____ problems people suffer from, and bipolar disorder is one of them. It can cause ❷ _____ swings in people and cause job and relationship problems, too. Some of its ❸ _____ are to make people think and talk ❹ _____ and to change their ❺ _____ instantly. Its causes could be a hormone ❻ _____ or lifestyle issues. To ❼ _____ it, people are encouraged to change their lifestyles and to take ❽ _____. People should reduce their stress, exercise, and sleep enough. Lithium can help, but people's symptoms ❾ _____ if they stop ❿ _____ it.

Unit 4 **Marketing Psychology**

Vocabulary

A **Read the sentences and choose the best words for the blanks.**

1 We will **market** our goods by _____ them online and in newspapers.

   a. sponsoring   b. making   c. improving   d. promoting

2 If you have good **intentions**, then you should be successful in your _____.

   a. reason   b. purpose   c. discussion   d. psychology

3 They used some **sophisticated** equipment, but even _____ machinery did not help.

   a. advanced   b. expensive   c. imported   d. old-fashioned

B **Choose the words from the box to complete the sentences.**

ploy	flocking	edge	cash register	impulsively

1 Customers are _____ to the store because of its big sale.

2 The store's marketing _____ is to offer discounts on many items.

3 There is a problem with the _____, so we cannot make any sales.

4 Some shoppers act _____ and buy things when they see them.

5 The café has a(n) _____ on its competitors because of its great marketing.

Translation

C **Read the sentences and translate them into your language.**

1 As more people purchase the items, they increase in popularity.

   → _____

2 Marketing refers to the art of convincing consumers to purchase a good or service.

   → _____

3 They often result in people flocking to them out of fear they will miss out on special deals.

   → _____

Paraphrasing

D **Paraphrase the sentences from the passage with the words and phrases in the box.**

employing	crucial	gain an advantage	be satisfied
are pleased	these days	often act rashly	using advanced methods

1 One important fact that psychologists know is that consumers tend to act impulsively.

→ One _____ fact psychologists know is that consumers _____.

2 By using marketing psychology, businesses hope to get an edge over their competition.

→ By _____ marketing psychology, businesses want to _____ over others.

3 Yet nowadays, some are resorting to more sophisticated methods by using marketing psychology.

→ But _____, some are _____ thanks to marketing psychology.

4 The message being sent is that if these people are happy, then other people will be happy by using the products as well.

→ The message is that if these people _____, then others will also _____ by using the products.

Listening

E **Listen to the summary and fill in the blanks.**

Some businesses use simple ❶ _____, but others use ❷ _____ methods by employing marketing psychology. Sellers try to understand their customers to gain an ❸ _____. For example, shoppers act ❹ _____, so stores place items for sale near cash registers. The ❺ _____ effect is also used. Ads show happy people using products, which makes others want to get on the bandwagon and ❻ _____ those items. ❼ _____ is another technique. It involves ❽ _____ a person something to make that person want to give something back. Stores use ❾ _____ to create feelings of scarcity and ❿ _____ as well.

Unit 5 Influenza

Vocabulary

A   Read the sentences and choose the best words for the blanks.

1   This animal has many **subtypes**, so there are several _____ of it in existence.

   a. kinds   b. sizes   c. colors   d. styles

2   There was an **outbreak** of the _____ in the countryside, and it killed many animals.

   a. vaccine   b. human   c. fighting   d. disease

3   Several types of **avian** diseases that come from _____ have been detected by scientists.

   a. bees   b. birds   c. cows   d. pigs

B   Choose the words from the box to complete the sentences.

originated	effectiveness	pandemic	virus	mortality rate

1   The _____ of this operation is very high.

2   Nobody knows where many diseases first _____.

3   In the fourteenth century, a(n) _____ killed millions of people in Europe.

4   The _____ in most countries has gotten lower due to advances in medicine.

5   You need a polio vaccination to prevent the polio _____ from making you sick.

Translation

C   Read the sentences and translate them into your language.

1   Three viruses—called the influenza A, B, and C viruses—are the causes of seasonal flu.

→ _____

2   Swine flu, for instance, is a combination of human, swine, and bird flu viruses.

→ _____

3   There are a total of sixteen H proteins and nine N proteins, which can combine to make numerous combinations of viruses.

→ _____

Paraphrasing

D **Paraphrase the sentences from the passage with the words and phrases in the box.**

are afraid	sickness	come from	form new types
get	come down with	huge numbers of	happens

1 One of the most common illnesses people catch is influenza, frequently called the flu.

→ Influenza, also known as the flu, is a common _____ people _____.

2 Experts fear it could someday cause a global pandemic that kills millions of people.

→ Experts _____ it might one day cause a global pandemic that kills _____ people.

3 The type of flu most people catch is called the seasonal flu because it only appears at certain times.

→ The kind of flu most people _____ is the seasonal flu since it only _____ at specific times.

4 The names are based on certain proteins which attach themselves to the influenza viruses and then create new forms of influenza.

→ The names _____ certain proteins that get attached to the flu viruses and then _____ of the flu.

Listening

E **Listen to the summary and fill in the blanks.**

Influenza is a common ❶ _____ many people catch. In the United States, people get ❷ _____ flu in winter. It ❸ _____ hundreds of thousands of people and kills tens of ❹ _____ of people ❺ _____. The influenza A, B, and C viruses cause seasonal flu. The A virus is serious and can cause ❻ _____. The B and C viruses are less ❼ _____. The A virus has several ❽ _____ because H proteins and N proteins can make new forms of influenza. ❾ _____ flu has sickened and killed large numbers of people. And ❿ _____ flu has a high mortality rate.

Unit 6 Nanotechnology and Medical Science

Vocabulary

A **Read the sentences and choose the best words for the blanks.**

1 The doctor will put some _____ into the patient's body by **injecting** them.

    a. food   b. fluids   c. solids   d. cells

2 The nurses will **monitor** the patient and closely _____ to make sure he gets healthy.

    a. learn   b. heal   c. understand   d. watch

3 The doctors will perform an **invasive** procedure when they _____ inside the patient's body.

    a. cut   b. look   c. put tubes   d. cure

B **Choose the words from the box to complete the sentences.**

cells	bloodstream	infancy	surgery	heal

1 Mr. Smith needs to have _____ to repair his knee.

2 There is some bacteria in the patient's _____.

3 Doctors believe they can _____ the patient with medicine.

4 The technology is in its _____ and is not well developed yet.

5 Cancer _____ are able to grow rapidly and cause harm to the body.

Translation

C **Read the sentences and translate them into your language.**

1 Nanotechnology involves the controlling of matter at a very small level.

   → _____

2 However, scientists and engineers are working hand in hand to develop nanorobots.

   → _____

3 For instance, some scientists hope to create nanorobots able to carry both a camera and medicine.

   → _____

Paraphrasing

D Paraphrase the sentences from the passage with the phrases in the box.

instruct the nanorobots	pain free	use methods	different industries
probably be used	most modern	contribute to	after detecting

1 They believe it will be helpful to the construction, textile, transportation, and food safety industries.

→ They think it will _____ a wide variety of _____.

2 Upon finding cancer cells, the doctors will order the nanorobots to inject medicine into those places.

→ _____ cancer cells, the doctors will _____ to inject medicine there.

3 Most cancer treatments today require procedures that attack all cells—both healthy and unhealthy ones.

→ _____ cancer treatments _____ attacking healthy and unhealthy cells.

4 In a few years, it is likely that they will be used to cure cancer and other diseases and to make surgery simple and painless.

→ Soon, they will _____ to cure cancer and other sicknesses and to make operations easy and _____.

Listening

E Listen to the summary and fill in the blanks.

Nanotechnology involves controlling ❶ _____ at a very small level. Scientists will use ❷ _____ in many industries, including construction, ❸ _____, and transportation. For medicine, scientists will make nanorobots that carry cameras and ❹ _____. The nanorobots will enter the ❺ _____, find the problem areas, and ❻ _____ medicine. They will be used to attack and kill ❼ _____ cells. They will also conduct ❽ _____ deep inside the body to make it simple and ❾ _____. Nanorobots cannot do these things yet, but ❿ _____ hope they will be able to do that in a few years.

Unit 7 The Extinction of Prehistoric Megafauna

Vocabulary

A **Read the sentences and choose the best words for the blanks.**

1 During **prehistoric** times, nobody recorded _____ since there was no writing.

    a. letters   b. songs   c. music   d. history

2 When new species **emerge**, they suddenly _____ and start reproducing.

    a. grow   b. get big   c. appear   d. migrate

3 Scientists can **speculate** why the woolly mammoth went extinct, but they are just _____.

    a. guessing   b. talking   c. researching   d. guaranteeing

B **Choose the words from the box to complete the sentences.**

overhunting	theory	defenses	outcompete	population explosion

1 Some animals have _____ such as claws and sharp teeth.

2 There was a(n) _____ of humans in the twentieth century.

3 Humans were able to _____ Neanderthals thousands of years ago.

4 Many animals, such as the dodo bird, have gone extinct due to _____.

5 One _____ is that the woolly mammoth died because the ice age ended.

Translation

C **Read the sentences and translate them into your language.**

1 During prehistoric times, there were large numbers of megafauna.

  → _____

2 Humans crossed this bridge and settled both North America and South America.

  → _____

3 In the struggle for survival, some species were not strong enough to succeed.

  → _____

Paraphrasing

D **Paraphrase the sentences from the passage with the words and phrases in the box.**

> knows precisely   killing   highly likely
> disappear   die out   went extinct   made it to

1 Nobody is sure exactly how or why these animals went extinct.

→ Nobody _____ what made these animals _____ .

2 Some megafauna had already gone extinct by the time humans reached North America though.

→ Some megafauna had already died when humans _____ North America though.

3 Overhunting by humans was likely a major cause of the extinction of these animals in North America.

→ Humans _____ too many animals were likely a major reason these animals _____ in North America.

4 In all likelihood, it was a combination of all three theories that caused the woolly mammoth and other large animals to go extinct.

→ It is _____ that a combination of all three theories made the woolly mammoth and other large animals _____ .

Listening

E **Listen to the summary and fill in the blanks.**

During ❶ _____ times, there were many megafauna, such as the woolly mammoth and the saber-toothed tiger. Many lived in North America, but they started going ❷ _____ around 60,000 years ago and ❸ _____ completely by 9000 B.C. ❹ _____ by humans was one reason. After humans crossed a land ❺ _____ connecting Asia and North America, they killed many animals. Diseases may have ❻ _____ others. And when the ice age ❼ _____ , the weather became warmer. There was a ❽ _____ explosion, so many large animals were ❾ _____ for food. A combination of all three ❿ _____ probably killed these animals.

Unit 8 Animal Hunting Methods

Vocabulary

A **Read the sentences and choose the best words for the blanks.**

1 The cat will **creep** up on the mouse with its body _____ the ground.

    a. away from   b. close to   c. under   d. off

2 When an animal **lunges**, it moves quickly _____ the prey it is attacking.

    a. around   b. over   c. toward   d. next to

3 The cheetah **stalked** its prey by following it _____ while hidden in the grass.

    a. slowly   b. for a long time   c. quickly   d. loudly

B **Choose the words from the box to complete the sentences.**

packs	pursuing	ambush	paralyze	consumed

1 The hyenas are _____ the zebra to try to kill it.

2 Many snakes can _____ animals by biting them.

3 Wolves hunt in _____, so they can kill very large animals.

4 The hungry animal _____ the entire body of the rabbit it killed.

5 Tigers often _____ animals by attacking them suddenly from behind.

Translation

C **Read the sentences and translate them into your language.**

1 Large numbers of insects and reptiles use poison or venom when hunting.

    → _____

2 The group attack is an effective method utilized by social animals such as lions and wolves.

    → _____

3 Ambush hunters must find a place to lie in wait for an animal to approach their position.

    → _____

Paraphrasing

D **Paraphrase the sentences from the passage with the words and phrases in the box.**

means	loses power	always succeed	even though
kill prey	enough to live	objective	the swiftest	work

1 Then, when it becomes weak, the orcas bite and kill their target.

→ Then, after it _____, the orcas bite and kill their _____.

2 When predators hunt other animals, called prey, they utilize several methods of attack.

→ When predators try to _____, they use several _____ of attack.

3 While they are not always successful, they enable predators to feed enough to survive.

→ _____ their methods do not always _____, predators are still able to eat _____.

4 Cheetahs, the fastest land animals, utilize this method but are not always successful because the prey they pursue can also run swiftly.

→ Cheetahs, _____ land animals, use this method but do not _____ since their prey can run fast, too.

Listening

E **Listen to the summary and fill in the blanks.**

Predators have several methods to kill prey. ❶ _____ hunters wait for animals to ❷ _____ their position and then attack it. Tigers, chameleons, snakes, and crocodiles use this method. ❸ _____ animals such as wolves and orcas use group ❹ _____. They work together to attack and kill animals. Big cats prefer to ❺ _____ and chase their prey. ❻ _____ may use their great speed to run after animals. Insects and ❼ _____ may use ❽ _____ or venom. It is ❾ _____ into the body of a prey animal, which gets ❿ _____ and can then be eaten.

Unit 9 Underground Bodies of Water

Vocabulary

A **Read the sentences and choose the best words for the blanks.**

1 The **channel** of the _____ is getting deeper and deeper each year.

    a. forest   b. desert   c. river   d. road

2 The **origin** of life is unknown since we do not know exactly when it _____.

    a. involved   b. changed   c. began   d. got stronger

3 Water is **seeping** into the house and will _____ cause a great amount of damage to it.

    a. slowly   b. strongly   c. soon   d. always

B **Choose the words from the box to complete the sentences.**

acres	crust	body	erode	eventually

1 Floods can _____ the land very quickly.

2 The river _____ flows all the way to the ocean.

3 The lake covers an area of more than twenty _____.

4 There are many underground rivers in the Earth's _____.

5 The Pacific Ocean is the largest _____ of water on the Earth.

Translation

C **Read the sentences and translate them into your language.**

1 Many rivers have their own ecosystems full of fish and plants.

  → _____

2 These rivers may be entirely underwater or may rise to the surface at some places.

  → _____

3 It is possible that this ocean contains three times more water than all of the Earth's oceans combined.

  → _____

Paraphrasing

D **Paraphrase the sentences from the passage with the phrases in the box.**

gets into	bodies of water	through the paths
do not know	flows into	break down	an enormous ocean

1 Water may erode limestone underground and then travel through the channels it creates.

→ Water may _____ limestone and then flow _____ it makes.

2 Scientists have also discovered that there is a huge ocean lying deep beneath the Earth's surface.

→ Scientists have found _____ deep underneath the ground.

3 They form when water on the surface seeps into the ground, where it eventually winds up in a cave.

→ They form when surface water _____ the ground and, over time, _____ a cave.

4 It is likely that many more underground lakes, rivers, and oceans exist, but people are not aware of them.

→ There are probably many more underground _____, but people _____ about them.

Listening

E **Listen to the summary and fill in the blanks.**

There are not only ❶ _____ of water on the Earth's surface but also ❷ _____ it. Lakes are the most common ❸ _____ bodies of water and often ❹ _____ in cave systems. They can rise and fall. And temporary ones may be dangerous to people during the rainy ❺ _____. There are both ❻ _____ and natural underground rivers. They flow through cave systems or through ❼ _____ they create. Some are entirely underwater whereas others may ❽ _____ to the surface. There is an ❾ _____ ocean beneath North America. It may have three times more water than all of the oceans on the surface ❿ _____.

Unit 10 Deserts and Their Features

Vocabulary

A **Read the sentences and choose the best words for the blanks.**

1 The **cactus** is a _____ that people can often see in deserts.

a. mammal b. plant c. reptile d. landform

2 **Periodic** rainfall happens in deserts, so it falls at _____ times.

a. many b. rare c. early d. regular

3 **Semiarid** places around the world do not get very much _____.

a. wind b. rainfall c. hot weather d. cold weather

B **Choose the words from the box to complete the sentences.**

soil	continent	landforms	gravel	precipitation

1 Not much _____ falls in any deserts.

2 Deserts and hills are two types of _____.

3 There are many countries in the _____ of Asia.

4 There is a lot of _____ on the ground in this desert.

5 The _____ in deserts is not good for growing most plants.

Translation

C **Read the sentences and translate them into your language.**

1 Some have sand whereas others have gravel or rocks on their surfaces.

→ _____

2 While none receives much rain or snow, they vary in temperature, soil, and plant life.

→ _____

3 There are four main types of deserts: subtropical, semiarid, coastal, and polar, and each has its own distinct characteristics.

→ _____

Paraphrasing

D **Paraphrase the sentences from the passage with the words and phrases in the box.**

but	comprise about	very salty soil	get low amounts
since	change temperatures	very large	day turns to night

1 Their soil tends to have a high salt content, so their plants normally have extensive root systems.

→ They have _____, so plants in them have _____ root systems.

2 They undergo temperature shifts of up to forty-five degrees Celsius between day and night.

→ They can _____ up to forty-five degrees Celsius when _____.

3 Deserts are among the most common ecosystems as they cover approximately twenty percent of the Earth's land surface.

→ Deserts are very common ecosystems _____ they _____ twenty percent of the planet's land surface.

4 While these areas are constantly covered with snow, they are considered deserts because they receive small amounts of precipitation annually.

→ These places are covered with snow all year, _____ they are deserts since they _____ of annual precipitation.

Listening

E **Listen to the summary and fill in the blanks.**

> There are four main types of deserts, and all of them get a small amount of ❶ _____
> precipitation. ❷ _____ deserts are hot and ❸ _____. They include
> the Sahara Desert and the Arabian Desert. ❹ _____ deserts get long, dry summers
> and can get cold in winter. They often have ❺ _____ growing in them.
> ❻ _____ deserts like the Atacama Desert are found along the ❼ _____
> of oceans. They can have cold winters and have ❽ _____ soil. ❾ _____
> deserts like Antarctica and the northern Arctic Desert are ❿ _____ with snow all
> year and get small amounts of precipitation.

Unit 11 **The Great Wall of China**

Vocabulary

A **Read the sentences and choose the best words for the blanks.**

1 The villagers **countered** the invaders by _____ them as hard as they could.

    a. yelling at   b. challenging   c. running from   d. fighting

2 The _____ on the **watchtower** are keeping an eye out for the enemy army.

    a. workers   b. builders   c. guards   d. villagers

3 The _____ came running out of their **barracks** when the alarm sounded.

    a. cooks   b. students   c. soldiers   d. horses

B **Choose the words from the box to complete the sentences.**

erect	stable	stretches	starvation	fortified

1 The soldiers could not get into the _____ building.

2 He will take the horse to the _____ to get some rest.

3 The country's border _____ for hundreds of kilometers.

4 It will take a few days to _____ a wall around the base.

5 They have not eaten in a couple of weeks, so they are dying of _____.

Translation

C **Read the sentences and translate them into your language.**

1 To counter their enemies, tribes began building walls.

   ➡ _____

2 At times, around one million soldiers protected China's northern frontier from its enemies.

   ➡ _____

3 Up to a million people may have died working on the wall because of accidents, exhaustion, disease, starvation, and animal attacks.

   ➡ _____

Paraphrasing

D **Paraphrase the sentences from the passage with the words and phrases in the box.**

beside	demanded	be built	in the world
go sightseeing	mostly made of	were used	buildings

1 Alongside the wall, there were barracks for soldiers and stables for horses.

→ _____ the wall were _____ for soldiers and stables for horses.

2 Qin Shi Huang, China's first emperor, ordered construction of a fortified wall.

→ The first emperor of China _____ that a strong wall _____.

3 Much of the Great Wall was initially constructed with earth, straw, and tree branches while stones were added later.

→ The Great Wall was first _____ earth, straw, and tree branches, but stones _____ later.

4 Nevertheless, large areas still exist, making it a popular tourist attraction, and it remains the world's longest manmade structure.

→ Still, large parts of it exist, so many people _____ there, and it is still the longest manmade structure _____.

Listening

E **Listen to the summary and fill in the blanks.**

> The Chinese started ❶ _____ the Great Wall of China in the ❷ _____
> century B.C. because of warring tribes. Qin Shi Huang, the first ❸ _____ of China,
> ❹ _____ on it, and so did the Ming Dynasty. The wall is around six meters wide on
> ❺ _____ and up to fifteen meters high. Earth, ❻ _____, tree branches,
> stones, and bricks were used to build it. Millions of people made the wall, and up to a million
> ❼ _____ in the process. The wall has various towers and other ❽ _____.
> Large parts of it still ❾ _____ today, but much of it is in ❿ _____.

Unit 12 **Gutenberg's Printing Press**

Vocabulary

A   **Read the sentences and choose the best words for the blanks.**

1   The group **split up**, so it _____ into several small groups of people.

   a. exploded   b. advanced   c. added   d. broke up

2   They **transmitted** a message and _____ it to many places in the country.

   a. sent   b. announced   c. sold   d. changed

3   The construction project is **underway**, so _____ is being made on the building.

   a. fundraising   b. progress   c. planning   d. designing

B   **Choose the words from the box to complete the sentences.**

dip	print run	ambitious	literacy rate	acquired

1   The _____ in Switzerland is nearly 100%.

2   The new novel has a _____ of 10,000 books.

3   The author is _____ and hopes to write a bestseller.

4   _____ the pieces into ink and then press them onto paper.

5   Angela _____ several new books at the bookstore yesterday.

Translation

C   **Read the sentences and translate them Into your language.**

1   Printing press technology rapidly spread throughout Europe.

   → _____

2   But the metal pieces Gutenberg used let him print pages much more quickly.

   → _____

3   People in cultures such as ancient Egypt, China, and India all developed writing systems, and they later spread around the world.

   → _____

Paraphrasing

D **Paraphrase the sentences from the passage with the words and phrases in the box.**

utilized	started inventing	buy them	first printing
allowed	greatly lowered	was completed	from place to place

1 He began working to develop a machine that would use movable type.

→ He _____ a machine that _____ movable type.

2 By 1455, he had finished the first print run of what would be called the Gutenberg Bible.

→ By 1455, the _____ of his Gutenberg Bible _____.

3 This dramatically decreased the prices of books, enabling the middle class to acquire them.

→ This _____ book prices, letting people in the middle class _____.

4 The printing press enabled the knowledge learned and relearned in this period to move elsewhere rapidly.

→ The printing press _____ the knowledge of the age to move _____ fast.

Listening

E **Listen to the summary and fill in the blanks.**

For thousands of years, ❶ _____ people could read and ❷ _____ because books were rare and ❸ _____ by hand. Then, Johannes Gutenberg invented a ❹ _____ press that used movable type. It used ❺ _____ pieces. His printing press could print thousands of pages a day. Gutenberg printed the Gutenberg Bible, and printing press technology ❻ _____ rapidly. Thanks to the printing press, more people ❼ _____ to read, and the ❽ _____ of the Renaissance and Reformation spread. Other later ❾ _____, such as the Age of Enlightenment and the Industrial ❿ _____, happened more quickly thanks to the printing press.

Unit 13 **Plant Diseases**

Vocabulary

A **Read the sentences and choose the best words for the blanks.**

1 He is **immune** to that disease so cannot be _____ by it.
   a. influenced   b. cured   c. harmed   d. touched

2 The **famine** is causing many problems in the country since there is no _____ anywhere.
   a. food   b. water   c. medicine   d. knowledge

3 Doctors found an **abnormality** in the cells and determined that something was _____.
   a. unusual   b. safe   c. tiny   d. large

B **Choose the words from the box to complete the sentences.**

devastating	bark	dormant	staple	strain

1 Scientists developed a new _____ of wheat.

2 Rice is a _____ in many countries in Asia.

3 The _____ of the tree is hard enough to keep it safe.

4 Some plant diseases are _____ and kill millions of plants.

5 The virus will be _____ until the conditions for it to grow exist.

Translation

C **Read the sentences and translate them into your language.**

1 Plant diseases can be caused by pathogens such as bacteria, viruses, and fungi.

   ➜ _____

2 A plant disease is any abnormality which disrupts the normal life of a plant.

   ➜ _____

3 Depending upon the type of disease, various parts of the plant may be attacked.

   ➜ _____

Paraphrasing

D **Paraphrase the sentences from the passage with the words and phrases in the box.**

	have evolved	took place	have devised ways
occurs	wiped out	bigger or reproduces	caused great problems

1 Over time, plants have developed ways to resist various diseases.

→ Over time, plants _____ to be able to resist various diseases.

2 Plants have developed various defenses, and humans have come up with ways to counter them as well.

→ Plants have developed defenses, and humans _____ to battle them, too.

3 This happened in the 1840s when a blight destroyed the staple potato crop in Ireland, which resulted in enormous problems there.

→ This _____ in the 1840s when a blight _____ the Irish potato crop, which _____ there.

4 The second stage happens when the pathogen lies dormant inside the plant for a certain period of time as it grows larger or multiplies in number.

→ The second stage _____ when the pathogen is dormant in the plant for a while as it gets _____ .

Listening

E **Listen to the summary and fill in the blanks.**

Pathogens can cause plants to catch ❶ _____ . These are any ❷ _____ that disrupt the normal lives of plants. Some diseases are ❸ _____ , but others, like the potato blight in Ireland in the 1840s, can be ❹ _____ . There are three main ❺ _____ of a plant disease. First, a pathogen ❻ _____ a plant. Next, the pathogen is ❼ _____ as it grows. Finally, symptoms appear on the plant. Plant diseases can affect ❽ _____ , the stem, leaves, or the bark of plants. Some plants have developed ways to ❾ _____ diseases while humans are using chemicals and developing disease-resistant ❿ _____ of plants.

Unit 14 **Hybrid Plants**

Vocabulary

A **Read the sentences and choose the best words for the blanks.**

1 He **attained** his goal, so he _____ money and fame.

a. spent   b. looked for   c. got   d. desired

2 By studying **genetics**, he learned all about the science of _____.

a. medicine   b. zoology   c. technology   d. heredity

3 A wide **variety** of plants live in rainforests, so there are many _____ of them.

a. types   b. styles   c. colors   d. appearances

B **Choose the words from the box to complete the sentences.**

crossbreed	tissue	trait	countless	robust

1 There are _____ diseases that affect plants and animals.

2 Some of that plant's _____ was damaged because of a disease.

3 One _____ of that plant is that it grows well in cold conditions.

4 The cactus is so _____ that it can survive in very hot and dry weather.

5 It is possible to _____ different types of apple trees with one another.

Translation

C **Read the sentences and translate them into your language.**

1 It is possible to crossbreed two varieties of the same species of plant to create a new one.

→ _____

2 Farmers began saving the seeds produced by those plants and planted them the following year.

→ _____

3 It was not until the late nineteenth century that people began understanding genetics though.

→ _____

Paraphrasing

D **Paraphrase the sentences from the passage with the words and phrases in the box.**

	brighter	everywhere	originates from	
information on		connecting it to	their crops	came to learn

1 The corn people eat around the world comes from a small plant originally found in Mexico.

→ The corn people _____ eat _____ a plant first found in Mexico.

2 This is done by taking a branch of one plant and attaching it to another plant already growing.

→ This is accomplished by taking a branch of a plant and _____ another plant that is growing.

3 Early farmers noticed that some plants they grew were bigger, stronger, more colorful, and more robust than others.

→ Early farmers saw that some of _____ were bigger, stronger, _____, and more robust than others.

4 His work became widely known, providing people with the knowledge needed to create hybrid plants.

→ People _____ about his work, which gave them _____ how to make hybrid plants.

Listening

E **Listen to the summary and fill in the blanks.**

Two varieties of the same ❶ _____ of plant can be ❷ _____ to create a hybrid plant. This can be ❸ _____ naturally or by people. Humans have been doing this ever since they learned how to ❹ _____. The ❺ _____ were not understood until Gregor Mendel crossbred pea plants. He showed people how to create ❻ _____. Some are created by taking ❼ _____ from one species and ❽ _____ it to a female plant of a different variety. It is also possible to ❾ _____ a branch of one plant onto another plant. There is a lot of plant ❿ _____ nowadays thanks to hybridization.

Unit 15 Water and Wind Currents

Vocabulary

A **Read the sentences and choose the best words for the blanks.**

1 The **rotation** of the Earth is what makes it _____.

a. turn around   b. create seasons   c. create wind   d. have gravity

2 The **circulating** water in the pond _____ from place to place.

a. follows   b. moves   c. sinks   d. rises

3 A **band** of rain is coming, so a small _____ of land will get precipitation.

a. farm   b. yard   c. town   d. strip

B **Choose the words from the box to complete the sentences.**

ripple	horizontally	parallel	salinity	interaction

1 Some currents move _____ to the shore.

2 There is a lot of _____ between wind and water.

3 Some winds move _____ while others move vertically.

4 The _____ of ocean water is much greater than that of lake water.

5 There was a small _____ in the lake when the boy threw a stone in it.

Translation

C **Read the sentences and translate them into your language.**

1 The Earth's rotation creates large areas of circulating winds in the upper atmosphere.

➜ _____

2 The rotation causes most currents to curve rather than to move in a straight line.

➜ _____

3 Currents are moving masses of air and water caused due to the interactions of various forces.

➜ _____

Paraphrasing

D **Paraphrase the sentences from the passage with the phrases in the box.**

comes into contact	exist far below	bodies of water
spinning of the Earth	are affected by	a strong stream

1 Wind currents are influenced by temperature, density, and the Earth's rotation.

→ Wind currents _____ temperature, density, and the _____.

2 Other ocean currents take place farther beneath the surface of the ocean.

→ Other ocean currents _____ the surface.

3 Most water currents happen in the world's oceans, but there are also currents in seas, rivers, and streams.

→ The oceans have the most water currents, but they exist in other _____, too.

4 When a large mass of heated air encounters very cold air high in the atmosphere, a powerful stream of moving air is created.

→ When lots of heated air _____ with freezing air high in the atmosphere, this makes _____ of moving air.

Listening

E **Listen to the summary and fill in the blanks.**

> Currents are moving ❶ _____ of air or water. Most water currents are in
> ❷ _____ and are most commonly near the surface. Other water currents may
> form deep ❸ _____ the surface of the ocean and may move ❹ _____
> or vertically. The Earth's ❺ _____ makes currents like the Gulf Stream Current
> ❻ _____ as they move. Wind currents are ❼ _____ by temperature,
> ❽ _____, air pressure, and the Earth's rotation. They form when air moves from
> high ❾ _____ areas to ones with low pressure. The jet stream is an air current high
> in the ❿ _____ that can move faster than 300 kilometers per hour.

Unit 16 Gravity in the Solar System

Vocabulary

A **Read the sentences and choose the best words for the blanks.**

1 These two **unequal** forces are _____ in strength.

a. similar   b. identical   c. different   d. great

2 **Asteroids** in the solar system are small objects that move around the _____.

a. gravity   b. comet   c. moon   d. sun

3 The _____ the Earth follows in its **orbit** of the sun takes 365 days to complete.

a. path   b. year   c. rotation   d. road

B **Choose the words from the box to complete the sentences.**

noticeable	exerts	tides	mass	maintains

1 The Earth _____ a gravitational pull over the moon.

2 The _____ rise and fall in part due to the moon's gravity.

3 Halley's Comet is usually _____ when it returns near Earth.

4 Gravity is the force that _____ moons in orbit around their planets.

5 The sun's _____ is much greater than all of the planets in the solar system combined.

Translation

C **Read the sentences and translate them into your language.**

1 Jupiter is huge, so its gravity is approximately 2.5 times that of Earth's.

➜ _____

2 The moon also has gravity, yet its gravity is equal to roughly one-sixth of Earth's.

➜ _____

3 While small objects have gravity, the pull they exert on other objects is so tiny that it cannot be measured.

➜ _____

Paraphrasing

D **Paraphrase the sentences from the passage with the words and phrases in the box.**

operates	exert a pull	calculating	large bodies of water
unseen	by their shores	the majority of	in their orbits

1 Gravity works the same way, so it is easy to measure and to understand its effects.

→ Gravity _____ the same way, so _____ and understanding its effects are simple.

2 Gravity is an invisible force of attraction that pulls all objects in the universe toward one another.

→ Gravity is an _____ force of attraction that makes all objects _____ toward one another.

3 Their gravity pulls at the oceans, seas, and some lakes, causing water to rise and fall along shorelines.

→ Their gravity pulls at _____ and makes the water rise and fall _____.

4 Most other planets in the solar system have moons, all of which are maintained in orbit by their planets' gravitational forces.

→ _____ the planets in the solar system have moons, and their planets' gravity keeps them _____.

Listening

E **Listen to the summary and fill in the blanks.**

Gravity is the force of ❶ _____ that makes objects ❷ _____ one another toward them. Its ❸ _____ are noticeable for large objects. Earth's gravity keeps the moon in ❹ _____ around it while the moon's gravity affects the ❺ _____ on the Earth. Moons are ❻ _____ in orbit by the gravitational forces of the planets that they go around. The gravity of each planet ❼ _____ in ❽ _____ and is determined by its mass and ❾ _____. Mercury and Venus have gravity weaker than ❿ _____, but Jupiter's gravity is 2.5 times greater than Earth's.

Further
Writing Practice

Unit 1 How Movies Affect Culture

What is an influential creative work that you know? What is it, and how has it affected culture?

A The following table shows some ideas for answering the question above. Check the one that you like the most. If you have your own idea, write it in the last row.

Creative Work	Effects on Culture
☐ Mona Lisa	• It is a famous painting made by Leonardo da Vinci in the 1500s. • The painting has featured in countless books, movies, plays, ads, and other creative works. People have written stories about it, and numerous attempts to imitate it have been made.
☐ Romeo and Juliet	• It is a well-known drama written by William Shakespeare in the 1500s. • The play has influenced young people in love all around the world. Some people have imitated the lives and deaths of Romeo and Juliet.
☐ Harry Potter	• It is a bestselling young-adult fiction novel written by J.K. Rowling in the 1990s. • The book inspired millions of children around the world to start reading books. Many of them read the seven books in the *Harry Potter* series and then started reading other books in the same genre.

B Use one of the ideas in A and write a short paragraph by using the idea.

I know about _____. It is _____

_____.

The work _____

_____

_____.

Unit 2 Painting Techniques of the Renaissance

Q **Who is a famous artist from the Renaissance? What is the artist's masterpiece? And what made the artist so great?**

A The following table shows some ideas for answering the question above. Check the one that you like the most. If you have your own idea, write it in the last row.

Artist	Masterpiece and Description
☐ Michelangelo	• His masterpiece is the sculpture *David*. • He is the greatest sculptor in history. He used a highly personal style that many artists tried to imitate. His paintings and sculptures have influenced many other artists.
☐ Botticelli	• His masterpiece is the painting *The Birth of Venus*. • He was a humanist painter and often painted religious and mythological scenes. He tried to capture beauty in the works he created.
☐ Raphael	• His masterpiece is the painting *The School of Athens*. • He painted various scenes from history. He was also able to show emotion in his works, which helped bring them to life.

B Use one of the ideas in A and write a short paragraph by using the idea.

One famous Renaissance artist is _____. His masterpiece _____
_____ .
He _____
_____
_____ .

Unit 3 Bipolar Disorder

Q **What is a common mental illness people suffer from? What are some of its symptoms?**

A The following table shows some ideas for answering the question above. Check the one that you like the most. If you have your own idea, write it in the last row.

Illness	Symptoms
☐ depression	• People with this illness feel sad almost all the time. • Sufferers may also be uninterested in various activities, feel guilty, have trouble falling asleep, and be unable to concentrate very much.
☐ schizophrenia	• People with this illness may see, hear, smell, or feel things nobody else does. • Sufferers may also have delusions, which are ideas that seem strange to others and are easy to prove wrong but make sense to sufferers.
☐ phobia	• People with this illness have an excessive fear of something. • Sufferers may experience anxiety when they are exposed to whatever they are afraid of. Others may faint or sweat excessively. Common fears are of small places, the dark, and snakes.

B Use one of the ideas in A and write a short paragraph by using the idea.

One common mental illness is _____. People _____

_____.

Sufferers may _____

_____

_____.

Unit 4 Marketing Psychology

What is a popular marketing method? How does it make people buy goods and services?

A The following table shows some ideas for answering the question above. Check the one that you like the most. If you have your own idea, write it in the last row.

Marketing Method	Features
☐ sale	• This method involves reducing the prices of various items for a certain amount of time. • This can attract new shoppers to the store. Those individuals might buy other products not on sale, and they might become regular shoppers at the store.
☐ special members club	• This method involves letting certain shoppers become members of a club that provides benefits. • This can give shoppers access to goods and services before nonmembers can buy them. Members can also get invited to various events and may get benefits such as reduced prices.
☐ free sample	• This method involves giving away a product to shoppers for free. • This can let shoppers try out a good before purchasing it. This is common at supermarkets and other food stores. Shoppers can taste the item and then determine if they want to buy it or not.

B Use one of the ideas in A and write a short paragraph by using the idea.

One marketing method is _____. This method _____
_____.
This can _____
_____
_____.

Unit 5 Influenza

What is a common illness people suffer from? What are some of its symptoms?

A   The following table shows some ideas for answering the question above. Check the one that you like the most. If you have your own idea, write it in the last row.

Illness	Symptoms
☐ cold	• People with a cold may have a runny or stuffy nose. • They may also have a sore throat, cough a lot, and sneeze. People with a cold may be sick for up to two weeks.
☐ stomachache	• People with a stomachache experience discomfort in the area around their stomach. • They may have sharp pain at times, and they may feel like they have to throw up, too.
☐ headache	• People with a headache have some type of pain in their head. • They may have sharp or dull pain that could last for several hours. Some people cannot concentrate or do routine activities when the pain is very great.

B   Use one of the ideas in A and write a short paragraph by using the idea.

One common illness is _____. People with _____
_____.
They _____
_____
_____.

Unit 6 Nanotechnology and Medical Science

Q **What is an industry that nanotechnology may influence in the future? How will it affect that industry?**

A The following table shows some ideas for answering the question above. Check the one that you like the most. If you have your own idea, write it in the last row.

Industry	Effects on the Industry
☐ manufacturing	• Nanotechnology could replace traditional manufacturing methods. • It will be able to create anything, which will lower the prices of items. This will make manufactured items cheap and plentiful.
☐ cosmetic surgery	• Nanotechnology could let people change their physical appearances. • It will let people change the shapes of their body parts without having to undergo any operations.
☐ textiles	• Nanotechnology could let clothes instantly change their appearance. • It will let a person wearing a T-shirt suddenly change it into a button-down shirt. People will be able to make any kinds of clothes they want with nanotechnology.

B Use one of the ideas in A and write a short paragraph by using the idea.

_____ is/are one industry that nanotechnology may influence in the future.

Nanotechnology could _____.

It will _____

_____.

Unit 7 The Extinction of Prehistoric Megafauna

What is an animal that went extinct in the past? Why did it die out?

A   The following table shows some ideas for answering the question above. Check the one that you like the most. If you have your own idea, write it in the last row.

Animal	Reasons for Extinction
☐ passenger pigeon	• This bird used to live in North America in great numbers. • People ate it as a cheap food, so billions of them were killed by hunters. The last passenger pigeon died in a zoo in 1914.
☐ Steller's sea cow	• This aquatic mammal lived in the waters of the North Pacific Ocean. • People were able to hunt this slow-moving and enormous animal easily. It was discovered in 1741 and went extinct within thirty years.
☐ Tyrannosaurus rex	• This enormous dinosaur lived on the land more than 65 million years ago. • It died when a huge asteroid hit the Earth. This caused a mass-extinction event that killed large amounts of life on the planet, including Tyrannosaurus rex.

B   Use one of the ideas in A and write a short paragraph by using the idea.

One animal that went extinct in the past is _____.

This _____.

The reason it died out is that _____

_____

_____

Unit 8 Animal Hunting Methods

Q   **What is an animal that hunts other animals? What hunting method does it use?**

A   The following table shows some ideas for answering the question above. Check the one that you like the most. If you have your own idea, write it in the last row.

Animal	Hunting Method
☐ frog	• It is an ambush hunter. It hunts for prey from both the land and the water. • It waits for prey such as an insect to come by. Then, it uses its long tongue to grab the prey and then eats it.
☐ lion	• It hunts in packs and usually hunts at night. • It moves stealthily toward its prey. When it is between ten and thirty meters of its prey, the lion and the other members of the pack will attack and try to catch it together.
☐ great white shark	• It hunts fish, seals, and other sea creatures by itself. • It often swims up toward the surface to attack its prey, such as a seal. It grabs the seal, leaps out of the water, and bites down on it, killing the seal.

B   Use one of the ideas in A and write a short paragraph by using the idea.

One animal that hunts others is _____. It _____

_____.

This animal _____

_____

_____.

Unit 9 **Underground Bodies of Water**

Q **What is an underground body of water you know about? Why is it notable?**

A The following table shows some ideas for answering the question above. Check the one that you like the most. If you have your own idea, write it in the last row.

Body of Water	Features
☐ the Lost Sea	• It is an underground lake found in the Craighead Caverns in the United States. • It is one of the world's largest underground lakes and has a surface more than 240 meters long. Nobody is sure exactly how large it is because it has not been fully explored.
☐ Mojave River	• It is a river that flows mostly underground in the Mojave Desert in the United States. • It flows above the ground in some places. However, most of the river flows under the surface from its source in the mountains to its end in a lake.
☐ Hamza River	• It is an enormous aquifer found in South America. • It flows more than 6,000 kilometers and is located around 4,000 meters deep. It flows beneath the Amazon Rainforest and flows into the Atlantic Ocean.

B Use one of the ideas in A and write a short paragraph by using the idea.

One underground body of water is _____. It _____

_____.

It _____

_____.

44

Unit 10 Deserts and Their Features

Q   **What is a well-known desert? Where is it located, and what are some of its features?**

A   The following table shows some ideas for answering the question above. Check the one that you like the most. If you have your own idea, write it in the last row.

Desert	Features
☐ Atacama Desert	• It is a coastal desert located on the Pacific coast of Chile. • One feature is that its soil is similar to that of the planet Mars. Another is that the desert is so dry that most high mountains there have no glaciers.
☐ Painted Desert	• It is a desert near the Grand Canyon in the United States. • One feature is that it undergoes extreme temperature changes. It can be from -30°C to more than 40°C. Another is that the landforms are colorful. They are shades of red, lavender, and other colors.
☐ Gobi Desert	• It is a cold desert located in both Mongolia and China. • One feature is that many fossils of extinct animals, including dinosaurs, have been found there. Another is that its desertification is responsible for some of the yellow dust that is a problem in Korea.

B   Use one of the ideas in A and write a short paragraph by using the idea.

One well-known desert is _____. It _____

_____.

One feature is _____

_____

_____.

Unit 11 The Great Wall of China

Q **What is an impressive structure built in the past? Who made it, and why was it made?**

A The following table shows some ideas for answering the question above. Check the one that you like the most. If you have your own idea, write it in the last row.

Structure	Characteristics
☐ Stonehenge	• This impressive structure is located near Salisbury, England. • It is a circle of enormous stones weighing several tons each. Nobody knows who made it between 3100 and 2480 B.C. It may have been made to be a calendar or an observatory.
☐ Pyramid of Giza	• This impressive structure is located near Cairo, Egypt. • It is a huge pyramid built by the Pharaoh Khufu between the years 2580 and 2560 B.C. It was made to be Khufu's tomb and was supposed to hold the treasures he would take to the afterlife.
☐ moai	• This is a stone statue that is found on Easter Island in the Pacific Ocean. • It stands between 2.5 and ten meters high. There are more than 1,000 moai and they were made by Polynesians around 1,000 years ago. They were made to honor the Polynesians' ancestors.

B Use one of the ideas in A and write a short paragraph by using the idea.

One of the most impressive structures I know is _____.

This _____.

It _____

_____

_____.

Unit 12 Gutenberg's Printing Press

Q **What is an invention that changed the world? What made it so influential?**

A The following table shows some ideas for answering the question above. Check the one that you like the most. If you have your own idea, write it in the last row.

Invention	Influence
☐ light bulb	• It changed people's living patterns. People no longer had to wake up when the sun rose and go to bed when the sun set. • Large power plants were built to bring electricity into people's homes, so it enabled people to get electric appliances in their homes.
☐ telephone	• It changed how people communicated. People no longer had to communicate face to face or by writing letters. • People could instantly communicate with others from hundreds or thousands of kilometers away. This let news spread very quickly.
☐ television	• It changed how people were entertained. People no longer had to go out to be entertained. • People could stay at their homes and watch TV shows and news programs. This enabled millions of people in a single country to have access to the same form of entertainment.

B Use one of the ideas in A and write a short paragraph by using the idea.

One invention that changed the world is _____.

It changed _____

_____.

In addition, _____

_____.

Unit 13 **Plant Diseases**

Q **What is a deadly disease that you know about? What are its symptoms?**

A The following table shows some ideas for answering the question above. Check the one that you like the most. If you have your own idea, write it in the last row.

Disease	Symptoms
☐ smallpox	• It is a highly infectious disease that killed hundreds of thousands of people a year until a vaccine for it was discovered. • People with it developed a rash on their bodies. People were very contagious at that time.
☐ bubonic plague	• It is a very dangerous disease that spreads through fleas. During the Middle Ages, it killed up to half of Europe's population. • People with it may have a fever, chills, and headaches. Parts of their bodies may become swollen, and places on their bodies may turn black.
☐ Ebola	• It is a highly contagious disease caused by a virus. Most people get it in places in Africa. • People with it may have a fever and fatigue. Later, they may start bleeding from various body parts, including their eyes, ear, nose, and internal organs.

B Use one of the ideas in A and write a short paragraph by using the idea.

I know about _____. It is _____

_____.

People with it _____

_____

_____.

Unit 14 **Hybrid Plants**

Q **What is a hybrid animal that you know? What two animals combined to create it? What are its characteristics?**

A   The following table shows some ideas for answering the question above. Check the one that you like the most. If you have your own idea, write it in the last row.

Animal	Characteristics
☐ zonkey	• It is a combination of a zebra and a donkey. • It has black and white stripes like a zebra on its legs. However, it has a head and ears like a donkey. It is an animal that cannot create any offspring of its own.
☐ geep	• It is a combination of a goat and a sheep. • It has wool like a sheep on some parts of its body. It has hair like a goat on other parts of its body. It is an artificial creation that is made in a lab.
☐ coywolf	• It is a combination of a coyote and a wolf. • It is larger in size than a coyote but smaller than a wolf. Since coyotes and wolves are closely related, they are born in the wild when a coyote and a wolf mate with each other.

B   Use one of the ideas in A and write a short paragraph by using the idea.

One hybrid animal I know is _____. It is a combination of _____
_____.

It _____
_____
_____.

Unit 15 **Water and Wind Currents**

Q **What is a force that can have a big effect on the Earth? In what ways can it affect the planet?**

A   The following table shows some ideas for answering the question above. Check the one that you like the most. If you have your own idea, write it in the last row.

Force	Effects
☐ plate tectonics	• There are seven major plates and many minor ones that make up the outer part of the Earth, which is the crust and part of the mantle. • These plates slowly move in different directions. Over time, they can change the way that the surface of the Earth looks.
☐ earthquake	• There are times when the movement of a plate or multiple plates can cause the earth to begin to shake. • An earthquake can cause cracks to appear in the land. It can change the paths of rivers and streams as well.
☐ glacier	• There are places on the Earth where snow remains all year long. The snow gets pressed down over time to form a glacier. • A glacier can move forward or backward. In doing so, it can erode the surface of the land. It can destroy mountains and form lakes.

B   Use one of the ideas in A and write a short paragraph by using the idea.

One force I know is _____. There are _____

_____ .

The way it affects the Earth is that _____

_____ .

Unit 16 Gravity in the Solar System

Q **What is a planet in the solar system you know about? What are some of its characteristics?**

A The following table shows some ideas for answering the question above. Check the one that you like the most. If you have your own idea, write it in the last row.

Planet	Characteristics
☐ Saturn	• It is the second-largest planet in the solar system and is a gas giant. • It has an extensive ring system surrounding it. In addition, it has at least eighty-two moons orbiting it.
☐ Jupiter	• It is the largest object in the solar system after the sun and is a gas giant. • It has a huge storm called the Great Red Spot on its surface. It has at least seventy-nine moons orbiting it.
☐ Mercury	• It is the smallest planet in the solar system and is a rocky planet. • It is the closest planet to the sun and takes only eighty-eight days to complete one orbit. However, it rotates slowly, so a day on Mercury lasts for fifty-eight Earth days.

B Use one of the ideas in A and write a short paragraph by using the idea.

One planet I know about is _____ . It is _____

_____ .

It _____

_____

_____ .

MEMO

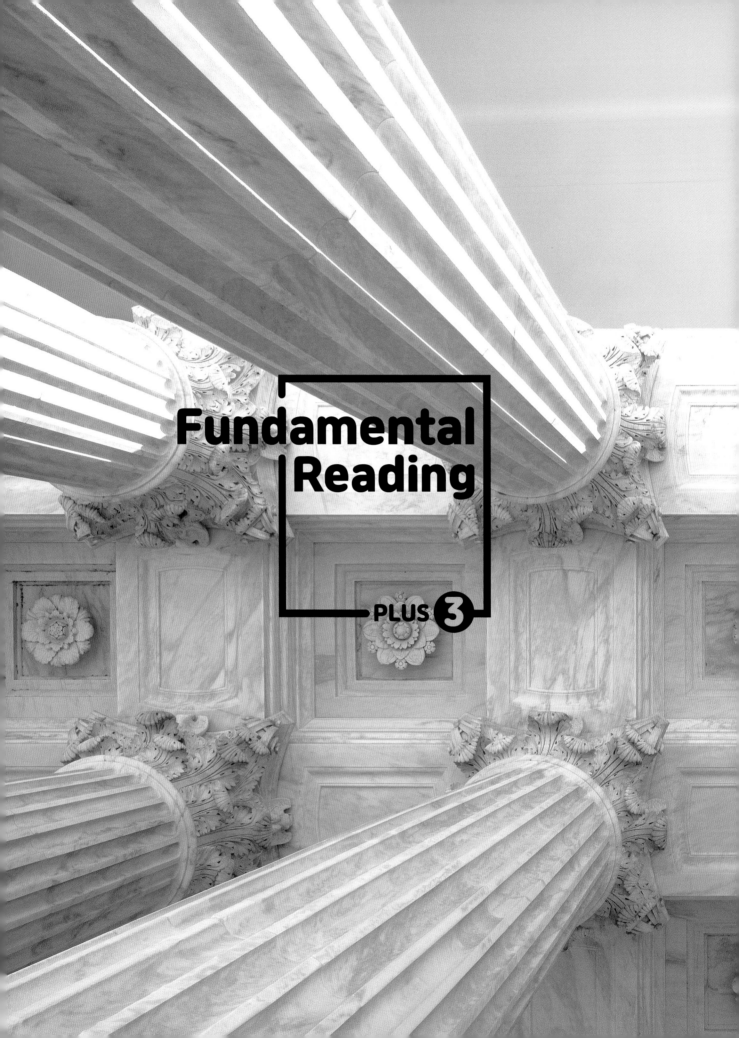

Fundamental Reading

PLUS 3